On Lying and Politics

HANNAH ARENDT

On Lying and Politics

Introduction by David Bromwich

A LIBRARY OF AMERICA
Special Publication

Library of Congress Control Number: 2022930517
ISBN 978–1–59853–731–4

3 5 7 9 10 8 6 4

Printed in the United States of America

Contents

INTRODUCTION

by David Bromwich

"TRUTHFULNESS HAS never been counted among the political virtues," Hannah Arendt asserts near the start of "Lying in Politics"; and she makes the same statement in almost the same words at the outset of "Truth and Politics." Lies, she adds, while never morally admirable, may be politically justifiable. This is an unsettling premise for the major essays Arendt would devote to the importance of truth in a free society. Her acceptance, however, of the fact that politicians lie comes from her understanding of the nature of a polity. Whether it takes the form of monarchy, oligarchy, or democracy, a polity is a regime in which people can live unmolested; and the typical activities of men and women are not mainly political, except at rare critical times in a democracy. A political lie, for Arendt, may therefore be justified, depending on the collective good it secures, since the largest duty of the leader or state official is simply to ensure the continuance of the society. But in a constitutional democracy, honest disclosure matters more than it does elsewhere. Here it is the self-understanding of the people that sustains the government. And as we enter the third decade of the twenty-first century—when the legitimacy of elections is widely challenged in America, on the basis of rumor, fantasy, and half-digested fact—we are living through one of those periods when conscientious record-keeping and the correction of error are both necessary and momentous. In the face of systematically deceptive leaders, democratic truth-telling shows a kind of integrity that does political work. It removes the stain and may restore the dignity of politics.

Arendt came to the attention of a wide public with the appearance in 1951 of *The Origins of Totalitarianism*. Totalitarian communism and Nazism alike were engendered by ideologists and cemented by the masses who went along with them. The governments and their compliant citizens acted from chosen facts or fictions about the world, and often a mystifying compound of fact and fiction. A salient feature of totalitarianism, as Arendt defined it, is the constant threat and frequent exercise of state power against foreign enemies but also "enemies of the state" within the society itself. The state, greatly expanded by a mesh of economic, cultural, and police bureaucracies, makes its presence felt with a certainty and intensity sufficient to burn away most traces and even memories of an older way of life. Totalitarian systems negate the very idea of a person. Russia under Stalin and Germany under Hitler in this sense embodied "radical evil"—leaving no space for the doubt, mixed feelings, and questions that are part and parcel of individual identity. The probable lifespan of a totalitarian system, it seemed to Arendt in 1951, was impossible to estimate, but there was clearly no outer limit.

Eichmann in Jerusalem: A Report on the Banality of Evil, published in 1963, marked a second statement and, to some extent, a revision of Arendt's view of totalitarianism. Adolf Eichmann was the high-ranking Nazi official who had arranged the procedures for transporting the Jews of Europe to the Nazi death camps. He was captured in 1960, in Argentina, by Israeli agents, and stood trial in Israel the following year for crimes against the Jewish people and crimes against humanity. Two aspects of Arendt's report on the trial were immediately noticeable to a close observer of her thinking. She had given up the thesis of radical evil: Eichmann, in court, had surprised her by his utterly commonplace nature, his addiction to cliché and apparent lack of zeal, indeed by a depthless ordinariness—which accounted for her use of the provocative word *banality*. On the other hand, his demeanor confirmed her view of the passive and morally unjudging creatures that were the offspring of mass society generally.[1] Not only those who obeyed but those who helped to invent and facilitate an evil as great as the mind could conceive might themselves be unremarkable. Far from the monsters in human form that fantasy likes to conjure up, they were conformists, careerists, hollow executors of a policy they could not think to question. (They might, of course, also have been enthusiasts, while the going was

good.) On this analysis, the most formidable administra-
tors of Nazi and Soviet communist terror resembled their
counterparts in luckier societies whose ability to judge an
evil system was never tested. Arendt's dry portrait of Eichmann was pitched outside the form of intellectual drama
many of her readers would have expected; and in writing of the destruction of the European Jews, she offered
a frank discussion of the policy of the Jewish councils.
For the councils themselves had cooperated with Nazi
authorities and thus ensured the peaceful dispossession
and deportation of their religious community. This part
of her account was felt by many to be lacking in sympathy
for the predicament of the councils; and the consequent
attacks on Arendt, especially by American Jewish organizations, prompted her to reflect on the imperviousness of
a group or a society faced with unpleasant truths.

Are lies then a latent hazard, or are they a usual condition of democracy itself? Lies to the people, the political theorist Uday Mehta has said in expounding Arendt,
"become the warrant for other lies." The people want to be
flattered; their leaders tell them what they want to hear—
that is one cause of lying. But "where security and the
unity of political society are foundational values, lies, like
violence, *always* have a conditional justification" because
"there is always some future eventuality with respect to
which a lie can be politically justified."[2] Lies claim permission within the ethic of responsibility about which Max
Weber wrote in "Politics as a Vocation." If I am a political

leader, I give the law not *to myself* but *on behalf of others*, with whatever fiction I require as the elected or appointed guardian of their security.

From the mid-1960s onward, Arendt's interest in the cooperation of democracy with lying was sharpened by the recurrent exposure of false claims of progress by American armed forces in the Vietnam War. These embarrassments reached their climax with the publication in March 1971 of the Pentagon Papers: a trove of classified documents, copied by a Rand Corporation scholar, Daniêl Ellsberg, that revealed a decade-long pattern of lies by the Johnson and Nixon administrations. This war—so the public had been told—was fought to prevent a communist takeover of Southeast Asia; and the official justifications often referred to the "domino theory": if one country went communist, all the others would follow. It emerged, however, from a reading of the Pentagon Papers that the foreign policy advisers under Johnson and Nixon, and going back as far as Kennedy and Eisenhower, had never given credence to the domino theory. Rather, the United States was in Vietnam—and was destroying the agricultural livelihood of the country even as it killed more than a million Vietnamese—largely in order to contain China. Yet the war went on, with false hopes of victory regularly conveyed, because getting out would mean a loss of face. The serial projections of success eventually became so penetrable that a euphemism was taken up by the mass media. The pattern was called the "credibility gap." The scandal of the Pentagon Papers was the proof they offered that the untruths emanating from government had been consciously fashioned.

The twin concerns outlined above—the manufacture of lies both under a totalitarian regime and in the apparently free public life of a corrupted democracy—may be seen to come together in "Truth and Politics" (1967) and "Lying in Politics" (1971). How much deception can we accommodate before we lose our self-understanding as responsible citizens? How do the lies change *us*? There is a tendency in all experience to make the strange somehow familiar, to normalize the abnormal. By this trick of the mind, state policies that were previously unthinkable can be rendered almost habitual. The expectation of privacy, for example—the confidence that there are a great many things about me that are known only if I want others to know them—is incomparably weaker now than it was for an American in 1950 or even 2000. The truth seems to be that our sociable instincts can enlist us as sudden collaborators in a revolutionary change. Since we have to coexist with our neighbors, it goes against the grain to suppose that the approved actions they agree to take are wrong; we may excuse a transgression that in ordinary circumstances we would find abhorrent; and eventually, we go along ourselves. If so many are doing it, how can it be very wrong? Arendt in her essays on lying suggests that this drift of behavior, multiplied many times in the conditions of modern democracy, can impair and finally destroy people's common sense of reality itself.

Often, in her writings, she alluded to Tocqueville's warning against the dangerous "omnipotence" of the opinions held by the majority in a democratic order; and she steadily emphasized the mischief of confusing opinion with knowledge. In no country, Tocqueville had said, are men so free as they are in the United States to do as they please, yet in no country is there less actual freedom of thought. The reason may be that people who know themselves to be equal as citizens expect to be on a level with their neighbors in all ways. Together with the demand of self-worth comes a natural anxiety about the opinions of their neighbors. It is as if they believed that their lives would stay normal and secure so long as everyone stayed the same. But at an exigent moment, as Tocqueville noted in his *Recollections*, such illusions of normal life can lead to a disastrous complacency in those who rule; in 1848, representatives of the old order in Europe resembled "the man who refused to believe that his house was on fire, because he had the key to it in his pocket."[3] Comfortable habit may find judgment asleep in the presence of extraordinary events.

The assimilation of the strange and monstrous to the familiar and tractable has an effect that goes deeper than politics. It cuts people off from their own experience. This *unexperiencing* relation to the world, in turn, makes them susceptible to further, stranger, more monstrous adaptations.[4] The exclusionist democracy of Athens and the elite republicanism of Rome were based on civic ideals that incorporated clearly demarcated lines of status. Those distinctions, supported by custom and tradition, acted as a curb on the pressure toward uniformity. A rights-based democracy like the United States can incorporate no such mechanism; and there are times when Arendt's admiration of high politics makes her a difficult friend for democracy. Yet she cherished a profound respect for the American constitutional founders, owing to the moral stature she discovered in their lives, the checks and limitations on power that their politics compelled, and above all their belief in representation as an alternative to simple majority rule. Indeed, the pattern of a desirable political life, for Arendt, was the New England town meeting. The participants in such an assembly, giving voice to their judgments about the public good, bear no comparison to the millions who look for and are granted access to the personal lives of citizens a thousand miles away. The invitation to imitative conformity has been scaled up—by social media, among other innovations—to such an extent that it betokens a change of kind rather than degree. And yet, if we follow Arendt's analysis, this was something always possible in human nature.

Eichmann, in his career as a Nazi bigwig, had perpetuated a state lie through action. He refined and administered a secret deadly policy against several million of his fellow human beings; and it was a policy based on a plain untruth: namely, that the presence of Jews in Europe threatened the substance of German society and the German nation, and that an international Jewish conspiracy was responsible for dragging America into the war. (It was the latter proposition—a fantasy that hardened into conviction in the mind of Hitler himself—that furnished the pretext for the Final Solution.) But Arendt asks us to realize that the Nazi lie, carried into action by persons incapable of moral judgment, differed from lesser lies only by the determination with which it was propagated and the atrociousness of the result. Lies, too, were deployed to justify the Soviet starvation policy in Ukraine in the 1930s, in order to assist certain larger communist aims: the collectivization of agriculture and the elimination of the Kulaks.

Something similar, with a less measurably vicious purpose at the top, occurred in the deceptive beginning and gradual moral degradation of American policy in Vietnam. By the early years of the Nixon administration, when Arendt examined the evidence, the public had long been aware of "free-fire zones" and the falseness of the body counts enforced by ambitious generals—the calculus by which a dead Vietnamese became automatically a Viet Cong. Here again Arendt recognized, but now close to home, the *limitless* character of public lies. They create a substitute world in which the truth is just one more opinion, and even this may not be their most surprising effect. For the officials who refine and repeat the lies eventually come to believe them, just as, in a social panic about "violence in the neighborhood," the person who first transmits the rumor and knows it to be exaggerated may come to share the panic with his hapless neighbors. Wishful thinking, too, is an inward form of lying. When it adds energy to a cause it knows to be questionable, there is still the pleasure of linking arms: a sensation agreeable enough to tamp down suspicion and nullify judgment.

The pattern of deception that launched, rationalized, and protracted the Vietnam War for a decade reappeared throughout the two decades of the Afghanistan War. In an exposure akin to Ellsberg's with the Pentagon Papers, the *Washington Post* reporter Craig Whitlock sued the government, under the Freedom of Information Act, to obtain the findings of the Special Inspector General for Afghanistan Reconstruction. Even in redacted form, the revelations were startling. Douglas Lute, "Afghanistan czar" for both the Bush and Obama administrations and the US ambassador to NATO from 2013 to 2017— an official as well placed as anyone to judge the pretensions of the US and its European allies—told his SIGAR interviewer in 2015: "We were devoid of a fundamental understanding of Afghanistan—we didn't know what we were doing." The details uncovered by Whitlock from the archive of such interviews are what might have been expected from the start. "Every data point was altered," an army colonel who served in 2013–14 is quoted as saying, in order "to present the best picture possible." The conclusion reached by John Sopko, the inspector general in charge of the survey, was that "the American people have been constantly lied to."[5]

More catastrophic in its result for the victim country was the conscious organization of untruths, misinterpreted facts, and speculations to rally political support for the Iraq War—an operation now known to have been desired by President George W. Bush previous to (and regardless of) the facts used to justify it. Here a compound of outdated reports of possible dangers was dressed up as an emergency peril of cataclysmic proportions. Fears, derived from mysterious violent deeds like the anthrax attacks in America that began a week after September 11, 2001, were easily linked in the popular mind to a familiar foreign source. Probably the most remarkable defection of conscience appeared in the work of the director of the CIA, George Tenet. In *To Start a War*, Robert Draper describes Tenet's code of conduct as follows: the CIA had somehow to "stay true to its mission" of reporting intelligence accurately "while maintaining . . . a posture of 'customer support'" for a president bent on war at all events. "Can we say," Tenet asked a CIA analyst at one meeting, "these three things [about Iraq and the terrorist network Al Qaeda]? There were some contacts. There was possibly some training. There was some haven." You could say so, replied the analyst, "But you should put it in context that these things add up to zero."[6] The final caveat never made it into the final report. Tenet gave the president to understand that speculative "facts," suitably abridged, were true; and the war-hungry president, knowing that he now had exactly the goods he wanted, conveyed a summary of pseudo-facts to the American people with no context whatsoever. Propaganda for the Iraq War also came in the form of sheer hypnotic repetition of the name of the internationally nonthreatening despot whom the president wanted to overthrow. By September 2002, George W. Bush was saying the name Saddam Hussein more often than he said Osama Bin Laden; and from this fact-free incantation as much as any other cause, he achieved the desired result: a majority of Americans believed that Saddam Hussein had worked with Al Qaeda to mount the attack on the U.S. on September 11, 2001. All this, at a time when the president, the vice president, the secretary of defense, and the secretary of state had been informed that the only purported evidence of a link between Iraq and Al Qaeda was thoroughly unreliable.

In both of her essays on truth and lie in politics, Arendt suggests that we consider lying an *activity*. Lying, after all, wants to alter reality, even though its medium is linguistic and not physical. "The blurring of the dividing line between factual truth and opinion," for Arendt, "belongs among the many forms that lying can assume, all of which are forms of action." And she goes further: the liar "is an actor by nature," since "he wants to change the world"; if the lie takes, people will hold new beliefs in consequence of the stories he told or the pseudo-facts he recited. The liar, then, possesses, curiously, a more definite motive to act than the inquirer after truth. His success will yield a measurable profit, and he indulges in the pursuit for just that reason. The unconditional teller of truth, by contrast, may have a hard time saying why he does what he does. This fascinating double portrait is consistent with Arendt's ambivalence regarding action itself. On the one hand, action is a necessity of all life, and public action is at the heart of political life. The classical tradition asks us to honor the "shining deed," whether committed by a fictive or a real hero; a leader such as Pericles is famous not only as an explainer of the common good, but also as a *doer*. On the other hand, Arendt shares with Kierkegaard a suspicion of action as such—action that, by its very nature, may work against the imagining of possibility. Act, and you contribute to make the world one thing rather than another thing; it is an adventure, a going-forth, an original creation; you have transformed intention into effect—but this involves a reduction, too, a loss that the satisfied actor is apt to lose sight of. And over time, as his actions are permitted or approved or imitated, the actor will forget and perhaps renounce the moral responsibility he bears as the doer. The ethic of action teaches that dynamism is its own reason for being. When linked to the ideology of progress, as it has been most plainly in the activities of modern science, it justifies what any earlier age would have judged a terrible

transgression: *acting into nature*. Arendt used that sug-
gestive and deliberately barbarous phrase in two contexts:
the experimental invention and wartime use of the atom
bomb, and the separation from Earth announced by the
"space race" of the late 1950s and early 1960s. There may
be, she suspects, a cosmic impiety in our willingness to
pass entirely outside the given world.[7] It is something like
destroying the world.

In a seemingly different register, Arendt points out that
lying is a quite commonplace form of political behavior.
Politicians, among others, lie in order to get a result, to
make their audience *do* or *refrain from doing* something
specific; and getting that result marks a pragmatic limit
to the liar's purpose. It is a shortcut to persuasion that the
facts alone would not allow. But having arrived at this
definition, Arendt goes a step beyond her idea of lying-
as-action. The fact that we can lie, she thinks, should not
be treated as a regrettable feature of our humanity. The
ability to lie gives an elemental proof of our freedom, in
a way that mere acceptance of an existing state of things
could never do. We must *decide* to lie, and it is this fact
that gives moral weight to the decision not to lie.

The essay "Lying in Politics" was eventually placed as
the first chapter in Arendt's last completed book, *Crises
of the Republic*, which looks back on the American social
upheaval of the 1960s and early 1970s—the rise of violence in cities, the civil rights and antiwar protests, the
loss of trust in government, police, and other forms of

domestic authority. These manifestations Arendt believes to have been intimately connected with the phenomenon of government lying. "The basic issue" brought forward by the Pentagon Papers, she says, "is deception." The impotence of the government in those years did not arise merely from rhetorical errors or the poorly supervised gathering of estimates. For there is always, Arendt believes, an inward relation between the "ability to change facts" and the "ability to act." When government changes the world behind the scenes—by concealing, distorting, or rendering inaccessible the facts of political conduct—it engages in a form of action. The consequent distortion of reality is an ever present danger, because no empirical statement about the world is exempt from doubt as "Two plus two equals four" is exempt. The liar has a jump on his audience; he is the performer and he takes the initiative. The liar in a democracy who operates with a political purpose, as we have seen, will tell the people what they want to hear. But in a democracy, too—and Arendt relishes the dramatic reversal—the liar is fated to become part of his audience. "The more people he has convinced, the more likely it is that he will end by believing his own lies."

The government officials who oversaw the Vietnam War "lived in a defactualized world anyway," says Arendt; and at first, therefore, they paid "no more attention to the fact that their audience refused to be convinced than to other facts." For this train of thought on "image-making" in the postwar decade, when politics and advertising came into closer relation than ever before, Arendt may have drawn upon Daniel Boorstin's book *The Image*. "We have come to believe in our own images," wrote Boorstin, "till we have projected ourselves out of this world."[8] The lies propagated by the Johnson and Nixon administrations to lengthen the war did not serve the public good of the U.S.; they only confirmed its image, and preservation of that image turns out to have been the strongest motive in extending and intensifying the war. The international credibility of the U.S. was said to depend on the American ability to make Vietnam a "test case" for the resolve of America "to have its way in world affairs"; accordingly, the enemy had to be hunted down and obliterated, from every jungle hamlet of the south to every industrial target of the north. What made this nullification of thought possible? Arendt calls the Pentagon strategists, and their think-tank associates and second-level technical help, "problem-solvers." One may be reminded of C. Wright Mills's characterization of the strategists who spoke of acceptable losses in nuclear war as "crackpot realists."[9] Even so, Arendt concludes, "defactualization and problem-solving were welcomed because disregard of reality was inherent in the policies and goals themselves." The lies were not broadcast to deceive the enemy but to comfort and pacify the audience at home.

The greater the improbability of an official explanation, the more pressing is the need to shore it up with unchecked reiterations, confirmations, enhancements.

So the kingdom of untruth expands, without bound-
ary or restraint. An officially sanctioned account of this
or that event is affirmed by bureaucratic oversight and
announced to the populace by a cooperative press and
media. A consensus is thereby established that floats
free of any concern with veracity. "To the extent," writes
Arendt, "to which unwelcome factual truths are tolerated
in free countries they are often, consciously or unconsciously, transformed into opinions." She noticed this
artificial creation of premature "facts," for example, in
the sudden consensus around the view that the assassination of John Kennedy was the work of a lone gun-
man. As late as 1999, it was possible for a reporter on a
major newspaper to suggest a story about a new cache
of JFK documents and be quizzed by a senior editor:
"What's your theory? What does this tell us about who
killed JFK?"—the implication being that such a story
would only be worth the effort if it solved the crime. The
double bind that regulates allowable information can be
seen here with unusual clarity. If you have a conspiracy
theory, you can safely be dismissed as paranoid. But if,
from a position of skeptical doubt, you ask permission to
look into new evidence for what it may reveal, the work
is considered useless.[10] The accepted "fact," no matter how
weakly defended, becomes an acceptable truth when it
promotes the smooth running of the machinery of consent. Explorations that cannot be thought of as "problem-
solving," because they do not deliver a clean solution, are

unwelcome. So the warranted criticism of spurious facts comes to be a process endlessly deferred.

Let us stand back and describe the larger tendency. A falsified present is created by government and its outworks in the media, in order to ease the acceptance of a future desired by the powerful. This perception might induce despair. Yet Arendt holds fast to the belief that nothing is finally lost of the knowable world:

> The trouble with lying and deceiving is that their efficiency depends entirely upon a clear notion of the truth that the liar and deceiver wishes to hide. In this sense, truth, even if it does not prevail in public, possesses an ineradicable priority over all falsehoods.[11]

Just as, in the Eichmann book, she gave up the idea of the totalitarian enforcer as the embodiment of radical evil, so here she clarifies her ultimate belief that a totalitarian system, contrary to her own fears, can never be sure it has walled off every human doubt that threatens its permanence. Skepticism is a faculty coeval with reason itself.

"Truth and Politics" and "Lying in Politics" differ greatly in their intellectual weight and approach. The former is a major philosophical statement, the latter a canny journalistic inquiry by a thoughtful citizen. These essays converge in their defense of a civic conscience whose exercise is a condition of intellectual liberty. "Truth and Politics" builds up to a major formulation of Arendt's moral psychology, and by the end, it seems to have articulated a kind of credo. Truth must be defended against politics, and nowhere more than in the conditions of modern democracy. Mass society adapts us to clichés about the dangers we ought to fear and the satisfactions we are expected to desire. These ideas, becoming part of our usual mental stock, alienate us from our own experience. That is part of what it means to be unable to think. For thinking is not the same as problem-solving, nor is it a process that yields a result, "the truth about X." Admittedly the misapprehension is common in the social sciences, as well as in the command performances of strategic thought. But how then shall we characterize genuine thinking? It is a commitment that leads where it may and never ends. "Truth," Arendt says (and she says it in many places and many ways), "is always the beginning of thought, thinking is always result-less."

To be alive to one's personal experience is a precondition of thinking; to stay open to the discoveries of thinking may require courage; and *political* courage "is indispensable because in politics not life but the world is at stake."[12] Yet, in America and the other commercial democracies, the culture of the image has flooded and suffused even private life; and this forgery of grown-up existence is mimed in the peer-group conformity of children. At an ever earlier age, the chatter and swarm of the group beseech the child; the consensus-hive is being molded, and with it a set of opinions that seem prior to and capable of overriding facts themselves. Mass culture makes a false reality of its favorite appearances. What Arendt called thinking is to a great extent the ability to recognize one's own experience as a thing apart from those appearances, and the willingness to use one's own experience in judging reality. Truth, thinking, and reality are mutually dependent concepts for Arendt; and in a climactic passage, "Truth and Politics" adds to their company a further encompassing term, the "common world."

That essay has begun by reminding us of the perishability of the common world—a world, that is, constituted not only of phenomena and sensations experienced by all in common, but also past events, regularities of nature, an inherited and internalized culture:

> Facts and events are infinitely more fragile things than axioms, discoveries, theories . . . produced by the human mind. The chances of factual truth surviving the onslaught of power are very slim indeed; it is always in danger of being maneuvered out of the world not only for a time but, potentially, forever.

Thus the preservation of facts from oblivion depends finally on an exertion of the will by the living generations. Arendt clarifies this warning by quoting Kant on the connection between individual experience, thinking, and freedom: "the external power that deprives man of the freedom to communicate his thoughts publicly, *deprives him at the same time of his freedom to think*." The italics are hers; and once again, it is the word "think" that she means to underline.

No matter how people may argue about the causes of the First World War, said Clemenceau, "they will not say Belgium invaded Germany." Arendt uses that statement to distinguish factual from rational truth. But we should not pass over lightly the value of agreement on facts, and agreement about where to find them. George Orwell anticipated Arendt in noticing an unprecedented danger here. He dramatized it in his novel *Nineteen Eighty-Four* and in a series of prescient essays of the 1940s, including "The Prevention of Literature," "Notes on Nationalism," and "Writers and Leviathan." Most remarkably, in a passage of "Looking Back on the Spanish War" he foreshadowed Arendt's argument:

> I am willing to believe that history is for the most part inaccurate and biased, but what is peculiar to our own age is the abandonment of the idea that history could be truthfully written. In the past people deliberately lied, or they unconsciously coloured what they wrote, or they struggled after the truth, well knowing that they must make many mistakes; but in each case they believed that "the

facts" existed and were more or less discoverable.
And in practice there was always a considerable
body of fact which would have been agreed to by
almost everyone. . . . It is just this common basis
of agreement, with its implication that human
beings are all one species of animal, that totalitarianism destroys. Nazi theory indeed specifically denies that such a thing as "the truth" exists.
There is, for instance, no such thing as "science."
There is only "German science," "Jewish science"
etc. The implied objective of this line of thought is
a nightmare world in which the Leader, or some
ruling clique, controls not only the future but the
past. . . . This prospect frightens me much more
than bombs.[13]

We can define the loss most simply by calling it a loss of
reality. As Arendt observes in a critical passage of "Truth
and Politics":

The surest long-term result of brainwashing is a
peculiar kind of cynicism—an absolute refusal to
believe in the truth of anything, no matter how
well this truth may be established. In other words,
the result of a consistent and total substitution of
lies for factual truth is not that the lies will now
be accepted as truth, and the truth be defamed as
lies, but that the sense by which we take our bear-

ings in the real world—and the category of truth vs. falsehood is among the mental means to this end—is being destroyed.

The preservation of factual truth matters because we have no substitute world to live in when this world is gone.

As elemental as factual truths are rational truths. Arendt's example is the famous affirmation by Socrates that "it is better to suffer wrong than to do wrong." The precept avows an unconditional duty not to support a social or personal wrong even if one's refusal might endanger oneself. Rational truths of this sort Arendt believes to be imperishable: they exist as truth apart from us. As one of her most sensitive commentators, Jerome Kohn, has pointed out, "necessary or rational truths" in her view "can be opposed by opinion, but they cannot be destroyed by lies; whereas factual truths . . . can be lied out of existence altogether." This is a reason for vigilance against the tyranny that democratic opinion may foster. Yet Arendt provokes us to reflect without complacency on human nature itself when she suggests that truth is naturally resented because it carries "an element of coercion." Tyrants have a quite comprehensible *motive* when they look with a jealous eye at the accessibility and deployment of truth. There is a power in truth that competes with their power. You cannot understand the truth and rationally wish to contradict it.

Arendt pours herself into the long second half of "Truth

and Politics." Always commanding our notice, in that extraordinary march of paragraphs, is the importance of having a footing in reality. We need this for the most practical of reasons: we want to commit ourselves to actions that are not utterly wrongheaded or self-deluded. Reading "Truth and Politics" after the chapters that precede it in Arendt's book *Between Past and Future,* one may feel that her sense of the common world means to connect human nature with physical nature. Her essay "The Crisis in Education" gives a more particular clue: "It seems to me that conservatism, in the sense of conservation, is of the essence of the educational activity, whose task is always to cherish and protect something—the child against the world, the world against the child, the new against the old, the old against the new." To be rooted in the given world prepares the child for the long work of self-invention—an adventure whose end can never be to acquiesce in the habits of that world: "Exactly for the sake of what is new and revolutionary in every child, education must be conservative."[14] In keeping with the same thought, one may conclude that Arendt judged her own work in the essays on lying and politics as provisionally conservative—that is to say, conservationist. These essays look to vindicate the reality of the common world, and they connect the present with a past whose survivals largely compose our understanding of the world.

Arendt taught for some years at the University of Chicago and later at the New School for Social Research—

institutions notable for their strong interest in political philosophy and the history of ideas. Having witnessed the rise of the Nazi ideology in Germany, she knew both the professional deformation to which scholars are liable and the political opportunism by which they can be tempted. Yet, by reason of her own experience, she regarded American universities as a bulwark against institutional lies. In 1970, in a conversation with Adelbert Reif, she avowed her belief that the chances for truth were "greatly improved by the mere existence of such places," which "make it possible for young people over a number of years *to stand outside all social groups and obligations,* to be truly free."[15] At the same time she confessed that the intolerance displayed in campus protests had partly shaken her trust: "in America, too, it is still conceivable that the universities will be destroyed, for the whole disturbance coincides . . . with an internal, not simply a political, crisis of the universities."[16] Arendt's doubts as well as her hope on this score had everything to do with her understanding of authority: the subject of an intricate essay in *Between Past and Future.* Authority, for her, denotes an imperative power of command that depends on neither force nor persuasion. Following authority is something people do without calculation, in view of their participation in a common world. "Where force is used, authority itself has failed," she writes; but authority likewise "is incompatible with persuasion. . . . Where arguments are used, authority is left in abeyance."[17] Scholarship may abort command and undo its own authority when it permits a user-friendly reference to "your truth" and "my truth"; as if, in relation to any event, decency required only a relaxed indifference, and no ill effects could issue from your truth and my truth being contradictory.

If one does care enough about truth to correct untruth, what should be the consequences for everyday conduct? This is the question that Arendt asks in the central passage of "Truth and Politics," and her answer should not surprise us by its radicalism. It is moral consistency that makes the individual person a single undivided being, a living force that is not exchangeable with any other:

> It is better [for the thinking person] to be at odds with the whole world than to be at odds with and contradicted by himself. . . . In other words, since man contains within himself a partner from whom he can never win release, he will be better off not to live in company with a murderer or a liar.

When a given pattern of falsification has become general, the truthteller may turn out to be something more than a reliable witness. "Where everybody lies about everything of importance, the truthteller, whether he knows it or not, has begun to act." Paradoxically, despite the division she respected between the active and the contemplative life, Arendt means here to honor the *efficacy* of thinking. But she wants us to recognize that self-censorship is as much an enemy of thought as the censorship whose function is to protect the lies told by the powerful. The dimming or deletion of our own original perceptions may form part of the same corrosive process, and a part we tend to underrate. How then do we find the courage to speak against untruth? Arendt, who had a sure command of several languages, took her wisdom where she found it. "There's an English idiom, 'Stop and think.' Nobody can think unless he stops."[18]

Notes

1. George Kateb offers a cogent criticism of Arendt's decision to associate Eichmann's *inability to think* with the incapacity of the masses to understand and judge their own situation: "If the concept of being unable to think is extendable beyond Eichmann, then the idea of the masses seems not to do the work Arendt wants it to do in *The Origins of Totalitarianism*. On the assumption that the idea of masses cannot explain the readiness to acquiesce in or to commit atrocities, it is not an obscene leniency to ask that a psychologist as great as she show more generosity in understanding those who, because of their suffering, put their desperate hope in a false redeemer. Why call thoughtless murderers mass-men? Then, too, why call distressed people masses?"; see Kateb, *Hannah Arendt: Politics, Conscience, Evil* (Towata, NJ: Roman & Allanheld, 1984), pp. 73–74.

2. Uday Mehta, "Is Lying a Political Virtue?" lecture delivered at the Hannah Arendt Center, Bard College, 2011. https://vimeo.com/26995316.

3. J. P. Mayer, ed., *The Recollections of Alexis de Tocqueville,* trans. Alexander Teixeira de Mattos (New York: Meridian Books, 1959), p. 9.

4. "The distinction between true and false—the standards of thought—no longer exists," comments Elisabeth Young-Bruehl, "in a regime where people have lost the capacity for experiencing

the world and for thinking"; see Young-Bruehl and Jerome Kohn, "Truth, Lies, and Politics: A Conversation," in "Hannah Arendt's Centenary: Political and Philosophic Perspectives, Part II," *Social Research,* vol. 74, no. 4 (Winter 2007): 1053.

5. Craig Whitlock, "The Afghanistan Papers: At War with the Truth," *Washington Post,* December 9, 2019. https://www.washingtonpost.com/graphics/2019/investigations/afghanistan-papers/afghanistan-war-confidential-documents/. Whitlock's full account appears in his book *The Afghanistan Papers* (New York: Simon & Schuster, 2021).

6. Robert Draper, *To Start a War: How the Bush Administration Took America into Iraq* (New York: Penguin Press, 2020), p. 146.

7. This conviction Arendt shared with her philosophical colleague and friend Hans Jonas; see Jonas, *The Imperative of Responsibility: In Search of an Ethics for the Technological Age* (Chicago: University of Chicago Press, 1984), chs. 4–5. Earlier reflections on "acting into nature" may be found in Arendt, *The Human Condition,* Anchor edition (New York: Doubleday, 1958), Prologue, chs. 43–45.

8. Daniel J. Boorstin, *The Image; Or What Happened to the American Dream* (New York: Atheneum, 1962), p. 241.

9. C. Wright Mills, *The Causes of World War Three* (New York: Ballantine Books, 1960), ch. 13.

10. A letter by Arendt dated April 2, 1965, sympathizes with Mary McCarthy's wonder at how skeptics of the Warren Report on the assassination are classified as paranoid: "I agree that one needs no counter-theory to disbelieve in the case against Oswald. On the contrary, every counter-theory would make this disbelief suspect. As though one had an axe to grind instead of looking simply at the evidence or rather at the lack of it." See Carol Brightman, ed., *Between Friends: The Correspondence of Hannah Arendt and Mary McCarthy, 1949–1975* (New York: Harcourt Brace, 1995), pp. 176–77.

11. A perceptive scholar of Arendt, Corinne Enaudeau, has drawn the appropriate inference from this passage: "Against a fantasy ideology intent on imposing its future on history by reinventing the past, [Arendt] asserts the right to create the future through the acceptance of the past"; see Enaudeau, "Hannah Arendt: Politics, Opinion, Truth," in *Social Research,* "Political and Philosophic Perspectives, Part II," 1036.

12. "What Is Freedom?" in Hannah Arendt, *Between Past and Future:*

Eight Exercises in Political Thought (New York: Penguin Books, 1968), p. 155.

13. "Looking Back on the Spanish War," in *The Collected Essays, Journalism, and Letters of George Orwell,* ed. Sonia Orwell and Ian Angus, 4 vols. (New York: Harcourt Brace, 1968), vol. 2, pp. 258–59.

14. Arendt, *Between Past and Future,* pp. 188, 189.

15. Hannah Arendt, *Crises of the Republic* (New York: Harcourt Brace, 1972), p. 208.

16. Ibid.

17. *Between Past and Future,* p. 92.

18. Hannah Arendt, *Thinking Without a Banister: Essays in Understanding, 1953–1975,* ed. Jerome Kohn (New York: Harcourt Brace, 2018), p. 286.

On Lying and Politics

Truth and Politics*

I

THE SUBJECT of these reflections is a commonplace. No one has ever doubted that truth and politics are on rather bad terms with each other, and no one, as far as I know, has ever counted truthfulness among the political virtues. Lies have always been regarded as necessary and justifiable tools not only of the politician's or the demagogue's but also of the statesman's trade. Why is that so? And what does it mean for the nature and the dignity of the political realm, on one side, and for the nature and the dignity of truth and truthfulness, on the other? Is it of the very essence of truth to be impotent and of the

---

*This essay was caused by the so-called controversy after the publication of *Eichmann in Jerusalem*. Its aim is to clarify two different, though interconnected, issues of which I had not been aware before and whose importance seemed to transcend the occasion. The first concerns the question of whether it is always legitimate to tell the truth—did I believe without qualification in *"Fiat veritas, et pereat mundus"*? The second arose through the amazing amount of lies used in the "controversy"—lies about what I had written, on one hand, and about the facts I had reported, on the other. The following reflections try to come to grips with both issues. They may also serve as an example of what happens to a highly topical subject when it is drawn into that gap between past and future which is perhaps the proper habitat of all reflections.

very essence of power to be deceitful? And what kind of reality does truth possess if it is powerless in the public realm, which more than any other sphere of human life guarantees reality of existence to natal and mortal men— that is, to beings who know they have appeared out of non-being and will, after a short while, again disappear into it? Finally, is not impotent truth just as despicable as power that gives no heed to truth? These are uncomfortable questions, but they arise necessarily out of our current convictions in this matter.

What lends this commonplace its high plausibility can still be summed up in the old Latin adage "*Fiat iustitia, et pereat mundus*" ("Let justice be done though the world may perish"). Apart from its probable author in the sixteenth century (Ferdinand I, successor to Charles V), no one has used it except as a rhetorical question: Should justice be done if the world's survival is at stake? And the only great thinker who dared to go against the grain of the question was Immanuel Kant, who boldly explained that the "proverbial saying . . . means in simple language: 'Justice shall prevail, even though all the rascals in the world should perish as a result.'" Since men would not find it worth while to live in a world utterly deprived of justice, this "human right must be held sacred, regardless of how much sacrifice is required of the powers that be . . . regardless of what might be the physical consequences thereof."[1] But isn't this answer absurd? Doesn't the care for existence clearly precede everything else—every virtue and every principle? Is it not obvious that they become mere chimeras if the world, where alone they can be manifested, is in jeopardy? Wasn't the seventeenth century right when it almost unanimously declared that every commonwealth was duty bound to recognize, in Spinoza's words, "no higher law than the safety of [its] own realm"?[2] For surely every principle that transcends sheer existence can be put in the place of justice, and if we put truth in its place—"*Fiat veritas, et pereat mundus*"—the old saying sounds even more implausible. If we understand political action in terms of the means-end category, we may even come to the only seemingly paradoxical conclusion that lying can very well serve to establish or safeguard the conditions for the search after truth—as Hobbes, whose relentless logic never fails to carry arguments to those extremes where their absurdity becomes obvious, pointed out long ago.[3] And lies, since they are often used as substitutes for more violent means, are apt to be considered relatively harmless tools in the arsenal of political action.

Reconsidering the old Latin saying, it will therefore come as something of a surprise that the sacrifice of truth for the survival of the world would be more futile than the sacrifice of any other principle or virtue. For while we may refuse even to ask ourselves whether life would still be worth living in a world deprived of such notions as justice and freedom, the same, curiously, is not possible with respect to the seemingly so much less political idea of truth. What is at stake is survival, the perseverance in existence (*in suo esse perseverare*), and no human world destined to outlast the short life span of mortals within it will ever be able to survive without men willing to do what Herodotus was the first to undertake consciously— namely, λέγειν τὰ ἐόντα, to say what is. No permanence, no perseverance in existence, can even be conceived of without men willing to testify to what is and appears to them because it is.

The story of the conflict between truth and politics is an old and complicated one, and nothing would be gained by simplification or moral denunciation. Throughout history, the truth-seekers and truthtellers have been aware of the risks of their business; as long as they did not interfere with the course of the world, they were covered with ridicule, but he who forced his fellow-citizens to take him seriously by trying to set them free from falsehood and illusion was in danger of his life: "If they could lay hands on [such a] man . . . they would kill him," Plato says in the last sentence of the cave allegory. The Platonic conflict between truthteller and citizens cannot be explained by the Latin adage, or any of the later theories that, implicitly or explicitly, justify lying, among other transgressions, if the survival of the city is at stake. No enemy is mentioned in Plato's story; the many live peacefully in their cave among themselves, mere spectators of images, involved in no action and hence threatened by nobody. The members of this community have no reason whatever to regard truth and truthtellers as their worst enemies, and Plato offers no explanation of their perverse love of deception and falsehood. If we could confront him with one of his later colleagues in political philosophy—namely, with Hobbes, who held that only "such truth, as opposeth no man's profit, nor pleasure, is to all men welcome" (an obvious statement, which, however, he thought important enough to end his *Leviathan* with)—he might agree about profit and pleasure but not with the assertion that there existed any kind of truth welcome to all men. Hobbes, but not Plato, consoled himself with the existence of indifferent truth, with "subjects" about which "men care not"—e.g., with mathematical truth, "the doctrine of lines and figures" that "crosses no man's ambition, profit or lust." For, Hobbes wrote, "I doubt not, but if it had been a thing contrary to any man's right of dominion, or to the interest of men that have dominion, that the three angles of a triangle should be equal to two angles of a square; that doctrine should have been, if not disputed, yet by the burning of all books of geometry, suppressed, as far as he whom it concerned was able."[4]

No doubt, there is a decisive difference between Hobbes' mathematical axiom and the true standard for human conduct that Plato's philosopher is supposed to bring back from his journey into the sky of ideas, although Plato, who believed that mathematical truth opened the eyes of the mind to all truths, was not aware of it. Hobbes' example strikes us as relatively harmless; we are inclined to assume that the human mind will always be able to reproduce such axiomatic statements as "the three angles of a triangle should be equal to two angles of a square," and we conclude that "the burning of all books of geometry" would not be radically effective. The danger would be considerably greater with respect to scientific statements; had history taken a different turn, the whole modern scientific development from Galileo to Einstein might not have come to pass. And certainly the most vulnerable truth of this kind would be those highly differentiated and always unique thought trains—of which Plato's doctrine of ideas is an eminent example—whereby men, since time immemorial, have tried to think rationally beyond the limits of human knowledge.

The modern age, which believes that truth is neither given to nor disclosed to but produced by the human mind, has assigned, since Leibniz, mathematical, scientific, and philosophical truths to the common species of rational truth as distinguished from factual truth. I shall use this distinction for the sake of convenience without discussing its intrinsic legitimacy. Wanting to find out what injury political power is capable of inflicting upon truth, we look into these matters for political rather than philosophical reasons, and hence can afford to disregard the question of what truth is, and be content to take the word in the sense in which men commonly understand it. And if we now think of factual truths—of such modest verities as the role during the Russian Revolution of a man by the name of Trotsky, who appears in none of the

Soviet Russian history books—we at once become aware of how much more vulnerable they are than all the kinds of rational truth taken together. Moreover, since facts and events—the invariable outcome of men living and acting together—constitute the very texture of the political realm, it is, of course, factual truth that we are most concerned with here. Dominion (to speak Hobbes' language) when it attacks rational truth oversteps, as it were, its domain, while it gives battle on its own ground when it falsifies or lies away facts. The chances of factual truth surviving the onslaught of power are very slim indeed; it is always in danger of being maneuvered out of the world not only for a time but, potentially, forever. Facts and events are infinitely more fragile things than axioms, discoveries, theories—even the most wildly speculative ones—produced by the human mind; they occur in the field of the ever-changing affairs of men, in whose flux there is nothing more permanent than the admittedly relative permanence of the human mind's structure. Once they are lost, no rational effort will ever bring them back. Perhaps the chances that Euclidean mathematics or Einstein's theory of relativity—let alone Plato's philosophy—would have been reproduced in time if their authors had been prevented from handing them down to posterity are not very good either, yet they are infinitely better than the chances that a fact of importance, forgotten or, more likely, lied away, will one day be rediscovered.

II

Although the politically most relevant truths are factual, the conflict between truth and politics was first discovered and articulated with respect to rational truth. The opposite of a rationally true statement is either error and ignorance, as in the sciences, or illusion and opinion, as in philosophy. Deliberate falsehood, the plain lie, plays its role only in the domain of factual statements, and it seems significant, and rather odd, that in the long debate about this antagonism of truth and politics, from Plato to Hobbes, no one, apparently, ever believed that organized lying, as we know it today, could be an adequate weapon against truth. In Plato, the truthteller is in danger of his life, and in Hobbes, where he has become an author, he is threatened with the burning of his books; mere mendacity is not an issue. It is the sophist and the ignoramus rather than the liar who occupy Plato's thought, and where he distinguishes between error and lie—that is, between "involuntary and voluntary ψεῦδος"—he is, characteristically, much harsher on people "wallowing in swinish ignorance" than on liars.[5] Is this because organized lying, dominating the public realm, as distinguished from the private liar who tries his luck on his own hook, was still unknown? Or has this something to do with the striking fact that, except for Zoroastrianism, none of the major religions included lying as such, as distinguished from "bearing false witness," in their catalogues of grave sins?

Only with the rise of Puritan morality, coinciding with the rise of organized science, whose progress had to be assured on the firm ground of the absolute veracity and reliability of every scientist, were lies considered serious offenses.

However that may be, historically the conflict between truth and politics arose out of two diametrically opposed ways of life—the life of the philosopher, as interpreted first by Parmenides and then by Plato, and the way of life of the citizen. To the citizens' ever-changing opinions about human affairs, which themselves were in a state of constant flux, the philosopher opposed the truth about those things which in their very nature were everlasting and from which, therefore, principles could be derived to stabilize human affairs. Hence the opposite to truth was mere opinion, which was equated with illusion, and it was this degrading of opinion that gave the conflict its political poignancy; for opinion, and not truth, belongs among the indispensable prerequisites of all power. "All governments rest on opinion," James Madison said, and not even the most autocratic ruler or tyrant could ever rise to power, let alone keep it, without the support of those who are like-minded. By the same token, every claim in the sphere of human affairs to an absolute truth, whose validity needs no support from the side of opinion, strikes at the very roots of all politics and all governments. This antagonism between truth and opinion was further elaborated by Plato (especially in the *Gorgias*) as the antagonism between communicating in the form of "dialogue," which is the adequate speech for philosophical truth, and in the form of "rhetoric," by which the demagogue, as we would say today, persuades the multitude.

Traces of this original conflict can still be found in the earlier stages of the modern age, though hardly in the world we live in. In Hobbes, for instance, we still read of an opposition of two "contrary faculties": "solid reasoning" and "powerful eloquence," the former being "grounded upon principles of truth, the other upon opinions . . . and the passions and interests of men, which are different and mutable."[6] More than a century later, in the Age of Enlightenment, these traces have almost but not quite disappeared, and where the ancient antagonism still survives, the emphasis has shifted. In terms of pre-modern philosophy, Lessing's magnificent "*Sage jeder, was ihm Wahrheit dünkt, und die Wahrheit selbst sei Gott empfohlen*" ("Let each man say what he deems truth, and let truth itself be commended unto God") would have plainly signified, Man is not capable of truth, all his truths, alas, are δόξαι, mere opinions, whereas for Lessing it meant, on the contrary, Let us thank God that we don't know *the* truth. Even where the note of jubilation—the insight that for men, living in company, the inexhaustible richness of human discourse is infinitely more significant and meaningful than any One Truth could ever be—is absent, the awareness of the frailty of human reason has prevailed since the eighteenth century without giving rise to complaint or lamentation. We can find it in Kant's grandiose *Critique of Pure Reason*, in which reason is led to recognize its own limitations, as we hear it in the words of Madison, who more than once stressed that "the reason of man, like man himself, is timid and cautious when left alone, and acquires firmness and confidence in proportion to the number with which it is associated."[7] Considerations of this kind, much more than notions about the individual's right to self-expression, played a decisive part in the finally more or less successful struggle to obtain freedom of thought for the spoken and the printed word.

Thus Spinoza, who still believed in the infallibility of human reason and is often wrongly praised as a champion of free thought and speech, held that "every man is by indefeasible natural right the master of his own thoughts," that "every man's understanding is his own, and that brains are as diverse as palates," from which he concluded that "it is best to grant what cannot be abolished" and that laws prohibiting free thought can only result in "men thinking one thing and saying another," hence in "the corruption of good faith" and "the fostering of . . . perfidy." However, Spinoza nowhere demands freedom of speech, and the argument that human reason needs communication with others and therefore publicity for its own sake is conspicuous by its absence. He even counts man's need for communication, his inability to hide his thoughts and keep silent, among the "common failings" that the philosopher does not share.[8] Kant, on the contrary, stated that "the external power that deprives man of the freedom to communicate his thoughts publicly, *deprives him at the same time of his freedom to think*" (italics added), and that the only guarantee for "the correctness" of our thinking lies in that "we think, as it were, in community with others to whom we communicate our thoughts as they communicate theirs to us." Man's reason, being fallible, can function only if he can make "public use" of it, and this is equally true for those who, still in a state of "tutelage," are unable to use their minds "without the guidance of somebody else" and for the "scholar," who needs "the entire reading public" to examine and control his results.[9]

In this context, the question of numbers, mentioned by Madison, is of special importance. The shift from rational truth to opinion implies a shift from man in the singular to men in the plural, and this means a shift from a domain where, Madison says, nothing counts except the "solid reasoning" of one mind to a realm where "strength of opinion" is determined by the individual's reliance upon "the number which he supposes to have entertained the same opinions"—a number, incidentally, that is not necessarily limited to one's contemporaries. Madison still distinguishes this life in the plural, which is the life of the citizen, from the life of the philosopher, by whom such considerations "ought to be disregarded," but this distinction has no practical consequence, for "a nation of philosophers is as little to be expected as the philosophical race of kings wished for by Plato."[10] We may note in passing that the very notion of "a nation of philosophers" would have been a contradiction in terms for Plato, whose whole political philosophy, including its outspoken tyrannical traits, rests on the conviction that truth can be neither gained nor communicated among the many.

In the world we live in, the last traces of this ancient antagonism between the philosopher's truth and the opinions in the market place have disappeared. Neither the truth of revealed religion, which the political thinkers of the seventeenth century still treated as a major nuisance, nor the truth of the philosopher, disclosed to man in solitude, interferes any longer with the affairs of the world. In respect to the former, the separation of church and state has given us peace, and as to the latter, it ceased long ago to claim dominion—unless one takes the modern ideologies seriously as philosophies, which is difficult indeed since their adherents openly proclaim them to be political weapons and consider the whole question of truth and truthfulness irrelevant. Thinking in terms of the tradition, one may feel entitled to conclude from this state of affairs that the old conflict has finally been settled, and especially that its original cause, the clash of rational truth and opinion, has disappeared.

Strangely, however, this is not the case, for the clash of factual truth and politics, which we witness today on such a large scale, has—in some respects, at least—very similar traits. While probably no former time tolerated so many diverse opinions on religious or philosophical matters, factual truth, if it happens to oppose a given group's profit or pleasure, is greeted today with greater hostility than ever before. To be sure, state secrets have always existed; every government must classify certain information, withhold it from public notice, and he who reveals authentic secrets has always been treated as a traitor. With this I am not concerned here. The facts I have in mind are publicly known, and yet the same public that knows them can successfully, and often spontaneously, taboo their public discussion and treat them as though they were what they are not—namely, secrets. That their assertion then should prove as dangerous as, for instance, preaching atheism or some other heresy proved in former times seems a curious phenomenon, and its significance is enhanced when we find it also in countries that are ruled tyrannically by an ideological government. (Even in Hitler's Germany and Stalin's Russia it was more dangerous to talk about concentration and extermination camps, whose existence was no secret, than to hold and to utter "heretical" views on anti-Semitism, racism, and Communism.) What seems even more disturbing is that to the extent to which unwelcome factual truths are tolerated in free countries they are often, consciously or unconsciously, transformed into opinions—as though the fact of Germany's support of Hitler or of France's collapse before the German armies in 1940 or of Vatican policies during the Second World War were not a matter of historical record but a matter of opinion. Since such factual truths concern issues of immediate political relevance, there is more at stake here than the perhaps inevitable tension between two ways of life within the framework of a common and commonly recognized reality. What is at stake here is this common and factual reality itself, and this is indeed a political problem of the first order. And since factual truth, though it is so much less open to argument than philosophical truth, and so obviously within the grasp of everybody, seems often to suffer a similar fate when it is exposed in the market place—namely, to be countered not by lies and deliberate falsehoods but by opinion—it may be worth while to reopen the old and apparently obsolete question of truth versus opinion.

For, seen from the viewpoint of the truthteller, the tendency to transform fact into opinion, to blur the dividing line between them, is no less perplexing than the truthteller's older predicament, so vividly expressed in the cave allegory, in which the philosopher, upon his return from his solitary journey to the sky of everlasting ideas, tries to communicate his truth to the multitude, with the result that it disappears in the diversity of views, which to him are illusions, and is brought down to the uncertain level of opinion, so that now, back in the cave, truth itself appears in the guise of the δοκεῖ μοι ("it seems to me")—the very δόξαι he had hoped to leave behind once and for all. However, the reporter of factual truth is even worse off. He does not return from any journey into

regions beyond the realm of human affairs, and he cannot console himself with the thought that he has become
a stranger in this world. Similarly, we have no right to
console ourselves with the notion that his truth, if truth it
should be, is not of this world. If his simple factual statements are not accepted—truths seen and witnessed with
the eyes of the body, and not the eyes of the mind—the
suspicion arises that it may be in the nature of the political
realm to deny or pervert truth of every kind, as though
men were unable to come to terms with its unyielding,
blatant, unpersuasive stubbornness. If this should be the
case, things would look even more desperate than Plato
assumed, for Plato's truth, found and actualized in solitude, transcends, by definition, the realm of the many,
the world of human affairs. (One can understand that the
philosopher, in his isolation, yields to the temptation to
use his truth as a standard to be imposed upon human
affairs; that is, to equate the transcendence inherent in
philosophical truth with the altogether different kind
of "transcendence" by which yardsticks and other standards of measurement are separated from the multitude
of objects they are to measure, and one can equally well
understand that the multitude will resist this standard,
since it is actually derived from a sphere that is foreign to
the realm of human affairs and whose connection with it
can be justified only by a confusion.) Philosophical truth,
when it enters the market place, changes its nature and
becomes opinion, because a veritable μετάβασις εἰς ἄλλο

γένος, a shifting not merely from one kind of reasoning to another but from one way of human existence to another, has taken place.

Factual truth, on the contrary, is always related to other people: it concerns events and circumstances in which many are involved; it is established by witnesses and depends upon testimony; it exists only to the extent that it is spoken about, even if it occurs in the domain of privacy. It is political by nature. Facts and opinions, though they must be kept apart, are not antagonistic to each other; they belong to the same realm. Facts inform opinions, and opinions, inspired by different interests and passions, can differ widely and still be legitimate as long as they respect factual truth. Freedom of opinion is a farce unless factual information is guaranteed and the facts themselves are not in dispute. In other words, factual truth informs political thought just as rational truth informs philosophical speculation.

But do facts, independent of opinion and interpretation, exist at all? Have not generations of historians and philosophers of history demonstrated the impossibility of ascertaining facts without interpretation, since they must first be picked out of a chaos of sheer happenings (and the principles of choice are surely not factual data) and then be fitted into a story that can be told only in a certain perspective, which has nothing to do with the original occurrence? No doubt these and a great many more perplexities inherent in the historical sciences are real, but they are no argument against the existence of factual matter, nor can they serve as a justification for blurring the dividing lines between fact, opinion, and interpretation, or as an excuse for the historian to manipulate facts as he pleases. Even if we admit that every generation has the right to write its own history, we admit no more than that it has the right to rearrange the facts in accordance with its own perspective; we don't admit the right to touch the factual matter itself. To illustrate this point, and as an excuse for not pursuing this issue any further: During the twenties, so a story goes, Clemenceau, shortly before his death, found himself engaged in a friendly talk with a representative of the Weimar Republic on the question of guilt for the outbreak of the First World War. "What, in your opinion," Clemenceau was asked, "will future historians think of this troublesome and controversial issue?" He replied, "This I don't know. But I know for certain that they will not say Belgium invaded Germany." We are concerned here with brutally elementary data of this kind, whose indestructibility has been taken for granted even by the most extreme and most sophisticated believers in historicism.

It is true, considerably more than the whims of historians would be needed to eliminate from the record the fact that on the night of August 4, 1914, German troops crossed the frontier of Belgium; it would require no less than a power monopoly over the entire civilized world. But such a power monopoly is far from being inconceiv-

able, and it is not difficult to imagine what the fate of factual truth would be if power interests, national or social,
had the last say in these matters. Which brings us back to
our suspicion that it may be in the nature of the political
realm to be at war with truth in all its forms, and hence to
the question of why a commitment even to factual truth
is felt to be an anti-political attitude.

III

When I said that factual, as opposed to rational, truth
is not antagonistic to opinion, I stated a half-truth. All
truths—not only the various kinds of rational truth but
also factual truth—are opposed to opinion in their *mode
of asserting validity*. Truth carries within itself an element
of coercion, and the frequently tyrannical tendencies so
deplorably obvious among professional truthtellers may
be caused less by a failing of character than by the strain
of habitually living under a kind of compulsion. Statements such as "The three angles of a triangle are equal
to two angles of a square," "The earth moves around the
sun," "It is better to suffer wrong than to do wrong," "In
August 1914 Germany invaded Belgium" are very different in the way they are arrived at, but, once perceived
as true and pronounced to be so, they have in common
that they are beyond agreement, dispute, opinion, or consent. For those who accept them, they are not changed
by the numbers or lack of numbers who entertain the

same proposition; persuasion or dissuasion is useless, for the content of the statement is not of a persuasive nature but of a coercive one. (Thus Plato, in the *Timaeus*, draws a line between men capable of perceiving the truth and those who happen to hold right opinions. In the former, the organ for the perception of truth [νοῦς] is awakened through instruction, which of course implies inequality and can be said to be a mild form of coercion, whereas the latter had merely been persuaded. The views of the former, says Plato, are immovable, while the latter can always be persuaded to change their minds.[11]) What Mercier de la Rivière once remarked about mathematical truth applies to all kinds of truth: "*Euclide est un véritable despote; et les vérités géométriques qu'il nous a transmises, sont des lois véritablement despotiques.*" In much the same vein, Grotius, about a hundred years earlier, had insisted—when he wished to limit the power of the absolute prince—that "even God cannot cause two times two not to make four." He was invoking the compelling force of truth against political power; he was not interested in the implied limitation of divine omnipotence. These two remarks illustrate how truth looks in the purely political perspective, from the viewpoint of power, and the question is whether power could and should be checked not only by a constitution, a bill of rights, and by a multiplicity of powers, as in the system of checks and balances, in which, in Montesquieu's words, "*le pouvoir arrête le pouvoir*"—that is, by factors that arise out of and belong to the political realm proper—but by something that arises from without, has its source outside the political realm, and is as independent of the wishes and desires of the citizens as is the will of the worst tyrant.

Seen from the viewpoint of politics, truth has a despotic character. It is therefore hated by tyrants, who rightly fear the competition of a coercive force they cannot monopolize, and it enjoys a rather precarious status in the eyes of governments that rest on consent and abhor coercion. Facts are beyond agreement and consent, and all talk about them—all exchanges of opinion based on correct information—will contribute nothing to their establishment. Unwelcome opinion can be argued with, rejected, or compromised upon, but unwelcome facts possess an infuriating stubbornness that nothing can move except plain lies. The trouble is that factual truth, like all other truth, peremptorily claims to be acknowledged and precludes debate, and debate constitutes the very essence of political life. The modes of thought and communication that deal with truth, if seen from the political perspective, are necessarily domineering; they don't take into account other people's opinions, and taking these into account is the hallmark of all strictly political thinking.

Political thought is representative. I form an opinion by considering a given issue from different viewpoints, by making present to my mind the standpoints of those who are absent; that is, I represent them. This process of representation does not blindly adopt the actual views of those who stand somewhere else, and hence look upon the world from a different perspective; this is a question neither of empathy, as though I tried to be or to feel like somebody else, nor of counting noses and joining a majority but of being and thinking in my own identity where actually I am not. The more people's standpoints I have present in my mind while I am pondering a given issue, and the better I can imagine how I would feel and think if I were in their place, the stronger will be my capacity for representative thinking and the more valid my final conclusions, my opinion. (It is this capacity for an "enlarged mentality" that enables men to judge; as such, it was discovered by Kant in the first part of his *Critique of Judgment*, though he did not recognize the political and moral implications of his discovery.) The very process of opinion formation is determined by those in whose places somebody thinks and uses his own mind, and the only condition for this exertion of the imagination is disinterestedness, the liberation from one's own private interests. Hence, even if I shun all company or am completely isolated while forming an opinion, I am not simply together only with myself in the solitude of philosophical thought; I remain in this world of universal interdependence, where I can make myself the representative of everybody else. Of course, I can refuse to do this and form an opinion that takes only my own interests, or the interests of the group to which I belong, into account; nothing, indeed, is more common, even among highly sophisticated people, than the blind obstinacy that becomes manifest in lack of imagination and failure to judge. But the very quality of an opinion, as of a judgment, depends upon the degree of its impartiality.

No opinion is self-evident. In matters of opinion, but not in matters of truth, our thinking is truly discursive, running, as it were, from place to place, from one part of the world to another, through all kinds of conflicting views, until it finally ascends from these particularities to some impartial generality. Compared to this process, in which a particular issue is forced into the open that it may show itself from all sides, in every possible perspective, until it is flooded and made transparent by the full light of human comprehension, a statement of truth possesses a peculiar opaqueness. Rational truth enlightens human understanding, and factual truth must inform opinions, but these truths, though they are never obscure, are not transparent either, and it is in their very nature to withstand further elucidation, as it is in the nature of light to withstand enlightenment.

Nowhere, moreover, is this opacity more patent and more irritating than where we are confronted with facts and factual truth, for facts have no conclusive reason whatever for being what they are; they could always have been otherwise, and this annoying contingency is literally unlimited. It is because of the haphazardness of facts that pre-modern philosophy refused to take seriously the realm of human affairs, which is permeated by factuality, or to believe that any meaningful truth could ever be discovered in the "melancholy haphazardness" (Kant) of a sequence of events which constitutes the course of this world. Nor has any modern philosophy of history been able to make its peace with the intractable, unreasonable stubbornness of sheer factuality; modern philosophers have conjured up all kinds of necessity, from the dialectical necessity of a world spirit or of material conditions to the necessities of an allegedly unchangeable and known human nature, in order to cleanse the last vestiges of that apparently arbitrary "it might have been otherwise" (which is the price of freedom) from the only realm where men are truly free. It is true that in retrospect—that is, in historical perspective—every sequence of events looks as though it could not have happened otherwise, but this is an optical, or, rather, an existential, illusion: nothing could ever happen if reality did not kill, by definition, all the other potentialities originally inherent in any given situation.

In other words, factual truth is no more self-evident than opinion, and this may be among the reasons that opinion-holders find it relatively easy to discredit factual truth as just another opinion. Factual evidence, moreover, is established through testimony by eyewitnesses—notoriously unreliable—and by records, documents, and monuments, all of which can be suspected as forgeries. In the event of a dispute, only other witnesses but no third and higher instance can be invoked, and settlement is usually arrived at by way of a majority; that is, in the

same way as the settlement of opinion disputes—a wholly
unsatisfactory procedure, since there is nothing to prevent a majority of witnesses from being false witnesses.
On the contrary, under certain circumstances the feeling
of belonging to a majority may even encourage false testimony. In other words, to the extent that factual truth is
exposed to the hostility of opinion-holders, it is at least as
vulnerable as rational philosophical truth.

I observed before that in some respects the teller of
factual truth is worse off than Plato's philosopher—that
his truth has no transcendent origin and possesses not
even the relatively transcendent qualities of such political principles as freedom, justice, honor, and courage,
all of which may inspire, and then become manifest in,
human action. We shall now see that this disadvantage
has more serious consequences than we had thought;
namely, consequences that concern not only the person
of the truthteller but—more important—the chances for
his truth to survive. Inspiration of and manifestation in
human action may not be able to compete with the compelling evidence of truth, but they can compete, as we
shall see, with the persuasiveness inherent in opinion. I
took the Socratic proposition "It is better to suffer wrong
than to do wrong" as an example of a philosophical statement that concerns human conduct, and hence has political implications. My reason was partly that this sentence
has become the beginning of Western ethical thought,
and partly that, as far as I know, it has remained the only

ethical proposition that can be derived directly from the specifically philosophical experience. (Kant's categorical imperative, the only competitor in the field, could be stripped of its Judaeo-Christian ingredients, which account for its formulation as an imperative instead of a simple proposition. Its underlying principle is the axiom of non-contradiction—the thief contradicts himself because he wants to keep the stolen goods as his property—and this axiom owes its validity to the conditions of thought that Socrates was the first to discover.)

The Platonic dialogues tell us time and again how paradoxical the Socratic statement (a proposition, and not an imperative) sounded, how easily it stood refuted in the market place where opinion stands against opinion, and how incapable Socrates was of proving and demonstrating it to the satisfaction not of his adversaries alone but also of his friends and disciples. (The most dramatic of these passages can be found in the beginning of the *Republic*.[12] Socrates, having tried in vain to convince his adversary Thrasymachus that justice is better than injustice, is told by his disciples, Glaukon and Adeimantus, that his proof was far from convincing. Socrates admires their speeches: "There must indeed be some divine quality in your nature, if you can plead the cause of injustice so eloquently and still not be convinced yourselves that it is better than justice." In other words, they were convinced before the argument started, and all that was said to uphold the truth of the proposition not only failed to persuade the non-convinced but had not even the force to confirm their convictions.) Everything that can be said in its defense we find in the various Platonic dialogues. The chief argument states that for man, *being one*, it is better to be at odds with the whole world than to be at odds with and contradicted by himself[13]—an argument that is compelling indeed for the philosopher, whose thinking is characterized by Plato as a silent dialogue with himself, and whose existence therefore depends upon a constantly articulated intercourse with himself, a splitting-into-two of the one he nevertheless *is*; for a basic contradiction between the two partners who carry on the thinking dialogue would destroy the very conditions of philosophizing.[14] In other words, since man contains within himself a partner from whom he can never win release, he will be better off not to live in company with a murderer or a liar. Or, since thought is the silent dialogue carried on between me and myself, I must be careful to keep the integrity of this partner intact; for otherwise I shall surely lose the capacity for thought altogether.

To the philosopher—or, rather, to man insofar as he is a thinking being—this ethical proposition about doing and suffering wrong is no less compelling than mathematical truth. But to man insofar as he is a citizen, an acting being concerned with the world and the public welfare rather than with his own well-being—including, for instance, his "immortal soul" whose "health" should have precedence over the needs of a perishable body—the Socratic

statement is not true at all. The disastrous consequences
for any community that began in all earnest to follow ethical precepts derived from man in the singular—be they
Socratic or Platonic or Christian—have been frequently
pointed out. Long before Machiavelli recommended pro-
tecting the political realm against the undiluted principles of the Christian faith (those who refuse to resist evil
permit the wicked "to do as much evil as they please"),
Aristotle warned against giving philosophers any say in
political matters. (Men who for professional reasons must
be so unconcerned with "what is good for themselves"
cannot very well be trusted with what is good for others,
and least of all with the "common good," the down-to-
earth interests of the community.)[15]

Since philosophical truth concerns man in his singu-
larity, it is unpolitical by nature. If the philosopher nevertheless wishes his truth to prevail over the opinions of the
multitude, he will suffer defeat, and he is likely to conclude from this defeat that truth is impotent—a truism
that is just as meaningful as if the mathematician, unable
to square the circle, should deplore the fact that a circle is
not a square. He may then be tempted, like Plato, to win
the ear of some philosophically inclined tyrant, and in the
fortunately highly unlikely case of success he might erect
one of those tyrannies of "truth" which we know chiefly
from the various political utopias, and which, of course,
politically speaking, are as tyrannical as other forms of
despotism. In the slightly less unlikely event that his

truth should prevail without the help of violence, simply because men happen to concur in it, he would have won a Pyrrhic victory. For truth would then owe its prevalence not to its own compelling quality but to the agreement of the many, who might change their minds tomorrow and agree on something else; what had been philosophical truth would have become mere opinion.

Since, however, philosophical truth carries within itself an element of coercion, it may tempt the statesman under certain conditions, no less than the power of opinion may tempt the philosopher. Thus, in the Declaration of Independence, Jefferson declared certain "truths to be self-evident," because he wished to put the basic consent among the men of the Revolution beyond dispute and argument; like mathematical axioms, they should express "beliefs of men" that "depend not on their own will, but follow involuntarily the evidence proposed to their minds."[16] Yet by saying "*We hold* these truths to be self-evident," he conceded, albeit without becoming aware of it, that the statement "All men are created equal" is not self-evident but stands in need of agreement and consent—that equality, if it is to be politically relevant, is a matter of opinion, and not "the truth." There exist, on the other hand, philosophical or religious statements that correspond to this opinion—such as that all men are equal before God, or before death, or insofar as they all belong to the same species of *animal rationale*—but none of them was ever of any political or practical consequence, because the equalizer, whether God, or death, or nature, transcended and remained outside the realm in which human intercourse takes place. Such "truths" are not between men but above them, and nothing of the sort lies behind the modern or the ancient—especially the Greek—consent to equality. That all men are created equal is not self-evident nor can it be proved. We hold this opinion because freedom is possible only among equals, and we believe that the joys and gratifications of free company are to be preferred to the doubtful pleasures of holding dominion. Such preferences are politically of the greatest importance, and there are few things by which men are so profoundly distinguished from each other as by these. Their human quality, one is tempted to say, and certainly the quality of every kind of intercourse with them, depends upon such choices. Still, these are matters of opinion and not of truth—as Jefferson, much against his will, admitted. Their validity depends upon free agreement and consent; they are arrived at by discursive, representative thinking; and they are communicated by means of persuasion and dissuasion.

The Socratic proposition "It is better to suffer wrong than to do wrong" is not an opinion but claims to be truth, and though one may doubt that it ever had a direct political consequence, its impact upon practical conduct as an ethical precept is undeniable; only religious commandments, which are absolutely binding for the community of believers, can claim greater recognition. Does this fact not stand in clear contradiction to the generally accepted impotence of philosophical truth? And since we know from the Platonic dialogues how unpersuasive Socrates' statement remained for friend and foe alike whenever he tried to prove it, we must ask ourselves how it could ever have obtained its high degree of validity. Obviously, this has been due to a rather unusual kind of persuasion; Socrates decided to stake his life on this truth—to set an example, not when he appeared before the Athenian tribunal but when he refused to escape the death sentence. And this teaching by example is, indeed, the only form of "persuasion" that philosophical truth is capable of without perversion or distortion;[17] by the same token, philosophical truth can become "practical" and inspire action without violating the rules of the political realm only when it manages to become manifest in the guise of an example. This is the only chance for an ethical principle to be verified as well as validated. Thus, to verify, for instance, the notion of courage we may recall the example of Achilles, and to verify the notion of goodness we are inclined to think of Jesus of Nazareth or of St. Francis; these examples teach or persuade by inspiration, so that whenever we try to perform a deed of courage or of goodness it is as though we imitated someone else—the *imitatio Christi*, or whatever the case may be. It has often been remarked that, as Jefferson said, "a lively and lasting sense of filial duty is more effectually impressed on the mind of a son or daughter by reading *King Lear* than by all the dry volumes of ethics and divinity that ever were written,"[18] and that, as Kant said, "general precepts learned at the feet either of priests or philosophers, or even drawn from one's own resources, are never so efficacious as an example of virtue or holiness."[19] The reason, as Kant explains, is that we always need "intuitions . . . to verify the reality of our concepts." "If they are pure concepts of the understanding," such as the concept of the triangle, "the intuitions go by the name of schemata," such as the ideal triangle, perceived only by the eyes of the mind and yet indispensable to the recognition of all real triangles; if, however, the concepts are practical, relating to con- duct, "the intuitions are called *examples*."[20] And, unlike the schemata, which our mind produces of its own accord by means of the imagination, these examples derive from history and poetry, through which, as Jefferson pointed out, an altogether different "field of imagination is laid open to our use."

This transformation of a theoretical or speculative statement into exemplary truth—a transformation of which only moral philosophy is capable—is a borderline experience for the philosopher: by setting an example and "persuading" the multitude in the only way open to him, he has begun to act. Today, when hardly any philo- sophical statement, no matter how daring, will be taken seriously enough to endanger the philosopher's life, even this rare chance of having a philosophical truth politi- cally validated has disappeared. In our context, however, it is important to notice that such a possibility does exist for the teller of rational truth; for it does not exist under any circumstances for the teller of factual truth, who in this respect, as in other respects, is worse off. Not only do factual statements contain no principles upon which men might act and which thus could become manifest in the world; their very content defies this kind of verification. A teller of factual truth, in the unlikely event that he wished to stake his life on a particular fact, would achieve a kind of miscarriage. What would become manifest in his act would be his courage or, perhaps, his stubbornness but neither the truth of what he had to say nor even his own truthfulness. For why shouldn't a liar stick to his lies with great courage, especially in politics, where he might be motivated by patriotism or some other kind of legitimate group partiality?

IV

The hallmark of factual truth is that its opposite is neither error nor illusion nor opinion, no one of which reflects upon personal truthfulness, but the deliberate falsehood, or lie. Error, of course, is possible, and even common, with respect to factual truth, in which case this kind of truth is in no way different from scientific or rational truth. But the point is that with respect to facts there exists another alternative, and this alternative, the deliberate falsehood, does not belong to the same species as propositions that, whether right or mistaken, intend no more than to say what is, or how something that is appears to me. A factual statement—Germany invaded Belgium in August 1914—acquires political implications only by being put in an interpretative context. But the opposite proposition, which Clemenceau, still unacquainted with the art of rewriting history, thought absurd, needs no context to be of political significance. It is clearly an attempt to change the record, and as such, it is a form of *action*. The same is true when the liar, lacking the power to make his falsehood stick, does not insist on the gospel truth of his statement but pretends that this is his "opinion," to which he claims his constitutional right. This is frequently done by subversive groups, and in a politically immature public the resulting confusion can be considerable. The blurring of the dividing line between factual truth and opinion belongs among the many forms that lying can assume, all of which are forms of action.

While the liar is a man of action, the truthteller, whether he tells rational or factual truth, most emphatically is not. If the teller of factual truth wants to play a political role, and therefore to be persuasive, he will, more often than not, go to considerable lengths to explain why his particular truth serves the best interests of some group. And, just as the philosopher wins a Pyrrhic victory when his truth becomes a dominant opinion among opinion-holders, the teller of factual truth, when he enters the political realm and identifies himself with some partial interest and power formation, compromises on the only quality that could have made his truth appear plausible, namely, his personal truthfulness, guaranteed by impartiality, integrity, independence. There is hardly a political figure more likely to arouse justified suspicion than the professional truthteller who has discovered some happy coincidence between truth and interest. The liar, on the contrary, needs no such doubtful accommodation to appear on the political scene; he has the great advantage that he always is, so to speak, already in the midst of it. He is an actor by nature; he says what is not so because he wants things to be different from what they are—that is, he wants to change the world. He takes advantage of the undeniable affinity of our capacity for action, for changing reality, with this mysterious faculty of ours that enables us to *say*, "The sun is shining," when it is raining cats and dogs. If we were as thoroughly conditioned in our behavior as some philosophies have wished us to be, we would never be able to accomplish this little miracle. In other words, our ability to lie—but not necessarily our ability to tell the truth—belongs among the few obvious, demonstrable data that confirm human freedom. That we can change the circumstances under which we live at all is because we are relatively free from them, and it is this freedom that is abused and perverted through mendacity. If it is the well-nigh irresistible temptation of the professional historian to fall into the trap of necessity and implicitly deny freedom of action, it is the almost equally irresistible

temptation of the professional politician to overestimate
the possibilities of this freedom and implicitly condone
the lying denial, or distortion of facts.

To be sure, as far as action is concerned, organized
lying is a marginal phenomenon, but the trouble is that
its opposite, the mere telling of facts, leads to no action
whatever; it even tends, under normal circumstances,
toward the acceptance of things as they are. (This, of
course, is not to deny that the disclosure of facts may be
legitimately used by political organizations or that, under
certain circumstances, factual matters brought to public attention will considerably encourage and strengthen
the claims of ethnic and social groups.) Truthfulness has
never been counted among the political virtues, because
it has little indeed to contribute to that change of the
world and of circumstances which is among the most
legitimate political activities. Only where a community
has embarked upon organized lying on principle, and
not only with respect to particulars, can truthfulness as
such, unsupported by the distorting forces of power and
interest, become a political factor of the first order. Where
everybody lies about everything of importance, the truthteller, whether he knows it or not, has begun to act; he,
too, has engaged himself in political business, for, in the
unlikely event that he survives, he has made a start toward
changing the world.

In this situation, however, he will again soon find himself at an annoying disadvantage. I mentioned earlier the

contingent character of facts, which could always have been otherwise, and which therefore possess by themselves no trace of self-evidence or plausibility for the human mind. Since the liar is free to fashion his "facts" to fit the profit and pleasure, or even the mere expectations, of his audience, the chances are that he will be more persuasive than the truthteller. Indeed, he will usually have plausibility on his side; his exposition will sound more logical, as it were, since the element of unexpectedness— one of the outstanding characteristics of all events—has mercifully disappeared. It is not only rational truth that, in the Hegelian phrase, stands common sense on its head; reality quite frequently offends the soundness of common-sense reasoning no less than it offends profit and pleasure.

We must now turn our attention to the relatively recent phenomenon of mass manipulation of fact and opinion as it has become evident in the rewriting of history, in image-making, and in actual government policy. The traditional political lie, so prominent in the history of diplomacy and statecraft, used to concern either true secrets—data that had never been made public—or intentions, which anyhow do not possess the same degree of reliability as accomplished facts; like everything that goes on merely inside ourselves, intentions are only potentialities, and what was intended to be a lie can always turn out to be true in the end. In contrast, the modern political lies deal efficiently with things that are not secrets at all but are known to practically everybody. This is obvious in the case of rewriting contemporary history under the eyes of those who witnessed it, but it is equally true in image-making of all sorts, in which, again, every known and established fact can be denied or neglected if it is likely to hurt the image; for an image, unlike an old-fashioned portrait, is supposed not to flatter reality but to offer a full-fledged substitute for it. And this substitute, because of modern techniques and the mass media, is, of course, much more in the public eye than the original ever was. We are finally confronted with highly respected statesmen who, like de Gaulle and Adenauer, have been able to build their basic policies on such evident non-facts as that France belongs among the victors of the last war and hence is one of the great powers, and "that the barbarism of National Socialism had affected only a relatively small percentage of the country."[21] All these lies, whether their authors know it or not, harbor an element of violence; organized lying always tends to destroy whatever it has decided to negate, although only totalitarian governments have consciously adopted lying as the first step to murder. When Trotsky learned that he had never played a role in the Russian Revolution, he must have known that his death warrant had been signed. Clearly, it is easier to eliminate a public figure from the record of history if at the same time he can be eliminated from the world of the living. In other words, the difference between the traditional lie and the modern lie will more often than not amount to the difference between hiding and destroying.

Moreover, the traditional lie concerned only particulars and was never meant to deceive literally everybody; it was directed at the enemy and was meant to deceive only him. These two limitations restricted the injury inflicted upon truth to such an extent that to us, in retrospect, it may appear almost harmless. Since facts always occur in a context, a particular lie—that is, a falsehood that makes no attempt to change the whole context—tears, as it were, a hole in the fabric of factuality. As every historian knows, one can spot a lie by noticing incongruities, holes, or the junctures of patched-up places. As long as the texture as a whole is kept intact, the lie will eventually show up as if of its own accord. The second limitation concerns those who are engaged in the business of deception. They used to belong to the restricted circle of statesmen and diplomats, who among themselves still knew and could preserve the truth. They were not likely to fall victims to their own falsehoods; they could deceive others without deceiving themselves. Both of these mitigating circumstances of the old art of lying are noticeably absent from the manipulation of facts that confronts us today.

What, then, is the significance of these limitations, and why are we justified in calling them mitigating circumstances? Why has self-deception become an indispensable tool in the trade of image-making, and why should it be worse, for the world as well as for the liar himself, if he is deceived by his own lies than if he merely deceives others? What better moral excuse could a liar offer than that his aversion to lying was so great that he had to convince himself before he could lie to others, that, like Antonio in *The Tempest*, he had to make "a sinner of his memory, To credit his own lie"? And, finally, and perhaps most disturbingly, if the modern political lies are so big that they require a complete rearrangement of the whole factual texture—the making of another reality, as it were, into which they will fit without seam, crack, or fissure, exactly as the facts fitted into their own original context—what prevents these new stories, images, and non-facts from becoming an adequate substitute for reality and factuality?

A medieval anecdote illustrates how difficult it can be to lie to others without lying to oneself. It is a story about what happened one night in a town on whose watchtower a sentry was on duty day and night to warn the people of the approach of the enemy. The sentry was a man given to practical jokes, and that night he sounded the alarm just in order to give the townsfolk a little scare. His success was overwhelming: everybody rushed to the walls and the last to rush was the sentry himself. The tale suggests to what extent our apprehension of reality is dependent upon our sharing the world with our fellow-men, and what strength of character is required to stick to anything, truth or lie, that is unshared. In other words, the more successful a liar is, the more likely it is that he will fall prey to his own fabrications. Furthermore, the self-deceived joker who proves to be in the same boat as his victims will appear vastly superior in trustworthiness to the cold-blooded liar who permits himself to enjoy his prank from without. Only self-deception is likely to create a semblance of truthfulness, and in a debate about facts the only persuasive factor that sometimes has a chance to prevail against pleasure, fear, and profit is personal appearance.

Current moral prejudice tends to be rather harsh in respect to cold-blooded lying, whereas the often highly developed art of self-deception is usually regarded with great tolerance and permissiveness. Among the few examples in literature that can be quoted against this current evaluation is the famous scene in the monastery at the beginning of *The Brothers Karamazov*. The father, an inveterate liar, asks the Staretz, "And what must I do to gain salvation?" and the Staretz replies, "Above all, never lie to yourself!" Dostoevski adds no explanation or elaboration. Arguments in support of the statement "It is better to lie to others than to deceive yourself" would have to point out that the cold-blooded liar remains aware of the distinction between truth and falsehood, so the truth he is hiding from others has not yet been maneuvered out of the world altogether; it has found its last refuge in him. The injury done to reality is neither complete nor final, and, by the same token, the injury done to the liar himself is not complete or final either. He lied, but he is not yet a liar. Both he and the world he deceived are not beyond "salvation"—to put it in the language of the Staretz.

Such completeness and potential finality, which were unknown to former times, are the dangers that arise out of the modern manipulation of facts. Even in the free world, where the government has not monopolized the power to decide and tell what factually is or is not, gigantic interest organizations have generalized a kind of *raison d'état* frame of mind such as was formerly restricted to the handling of foreign affairs and, in its worst excesses, to situations of clear and present danger. And national propaganda on the government level has learned more than a few tricks from business practices and Madison Avenue methods. Images made for domestic consumption, as distinguished from lies directed at a foreign adversary, can become a reality for everybody and first of all for the image-makers themselves, who while still in the act of preparing their "products" are overwhelmed by the mere thought of their victims' potential numbers. No doubt, the originators of the lying image who "inspire" the hidden persuaders still know that they want to deceive an enemy on the social or the national level, but the result is that a whole group of people, and even whole nations, may take their bearings from a web of deceptions to which their leaders wished to subject their opponents.

What then happens follows almost automatically. The main effort of both the deceived group and the deceivers themselves is likely to be directed toward keeping

the propaganda image intact, and this image is threatened less by the enemy and by real hostile interests than
by those inside the group itself who have managed to
escape its spell and insist on talking about facts or events
that do not fit the image. Contemporary history is full
of instances in which tellers of factual truth were felt to
be more dangerous, and even more hostile, than the real
opponents. These arguments against self-deception must
not be confused with the protests of "idealists," whatever
their merit, against lying as bad in principle and against
the age-old art of deceiving the enemy. Politically, the
point is that the modern art of self-deception is likely to
transform an outside matter into an inside issue, so that
an international or intergroup conflict boomerangs onto
the scene of domestic politics. The self-deceptions prac-
ticed on both sides in the period of the Cold War are too
many to enumerate, but obviously they are a case in point.
Conservative critics of mass democracy have frequently
outlined the dangers that this form of government brings
to international affairs—without, however, mentioning
the dangers peculiar to monarchies or oligarchies. The
strength of their arguments lies in the undeniable fact
that under fully democratic conditions deception without
self-deception is well-nigh impossible.

Under our present system of world-wide communication, covering a large number of independent nations, no
existing power is anywhere near great enough to make
its "image" foolproof. Therefore, images have a relatively

short life expectancy; they are likely to explode not only when the chips are down and reality makes its reappearance in public but even before this, for fragments of facts constantly disturb and throw out of gear the propaganda war between conflicting images. However, this is not the only way, or even the most significant way, in which reality takes its revenge on those who dare defy it. The life expectancy of images could hardly be significantly increased even under a world government or some other modern version of the Pax Romana. This is best illustrated by the relatively closed systems of totalitarian governments and one-party dictatorships, which are, of course, by far the most effective agencies in shielding ideologies and images from the impact of reality and truth. (And such correction of the record is never smooth sailing. We read in a memorandum of 1935 found in the Smolensk Archive about the countless difficulties besetting this kind of enterprise. What, for instance, "should be done with speeches by Zinoviev, Kamenev, Rykov, Bukharin, *et al.*, at Party Congresses, plenums of the Central Committee, in the Comintern, the Congress of Soviets, etc.? What of anthologies on Marxism . . . written or edited jointly by Lenin, Zinoviev, . . . and others? What of Lenin's writings edited by Kamenev? . . . What should be done in cases where Trotsky . . . had written an article in an issue of the *Communist International*? Should the whole number be confiscated?"[22] Puzzling questions indeed, to which the Archive contains no replies.) Their trouble is that they must constantly change the falsehoods they offer as a substitute for the real story; changing circumstances require the substitution of one history book for another, the replacement of pages in the encyclopedias and reference books, the disappearance of certain names in favor of others unknown or little known before. And though this continuing instability gives no indication of what the truth might be, it is itself an indication, and a powerful one, of the lying character of all public utterances concerning the factual world. It has frequently been noticed that the surest long-term result of brainwashing is a peculiar kind of cynicism—an absolute refusal to believe in the truth of anything, no matter how well this truth may be established. In other words, the result of a consistent and total substitution of lies for factual truth is not that the lies will now be accepted as truth, and the truth be defamed as lies, but that the sense by which we take our bearings in the real world—and the category of truth vs. falsehood is among the mental means to this end—is being destroyed.

And for this trouble there is no remedy. It is but the other side of the disturbing contingency of all factual reality. Since everything that has actually happened in the realm of human affairs could just as well have been otherwise, the possibilities for lying are boundless, and this boundlessness makes for self-defeat. Only the occasional liar will find it possible to stick to a particular falsehood with unwavering consistency; those who adjust images and stories to ever-changing circumstances will find themselves floating on the wide-open horizon of potentiality, drifting from one possibility to the next, unable to hold on to any one of their own fabrications. Far from achieving an adequate substitute for reality and factuality, they have transformed facts and events back into the potentiality out of which they originally appeared. And the surest sign of the factuality of facts and events is precisely this stubborn thereness, whose inherent contingency ultimately defies all attempts at conclusive explanation. The images, on the contrary, can always be explained and made plausible—this gives them their momentary advantage over factual truth—but they can never compete in stability with that which simply is because it happens to be thus and not otherwise. This is the reason that consistent lying, metaphorically speaking, pulls the ground from under our feet and provides no other ground on which to stand. (In the words of Montaigne, "If falsehood, like truth, had but one face, we should know better where we are, for we should then take for certain the opposite of what the liar tells us. But the reverse of truth has a thousand shapes and a boundless field.") The experience of a trembling wobbling motion of everything we rely on for our sense of direction and reality is among the most common and most vivid experiences of men under totalitarian rule.

Hence, the undeniable affinity of lying with action, with changing the world—in short, with politics—is limited by the very nature of the things that are open to man's faculty for action. The convinced image-maker is in error when he believes that he can anticipate changes by lying about factual matters that everybody wishes to eliminate anyhow. The erection of Potëmkin's villages, so dear to the politicians and propagandists of underdeveloped countries, never leads to the establishment of the real thing but only to a proliferation and perfection of make-believe. Not the past—and all factual truth, of course, concerns the past—or the present, insofar as it is the outcome of the past, but the future is open to action. If the past and present are treated as parts of the future—that is, changed back into their former state of potentiality—the political realm is deprived not only of its main stabilizing force but of the starting point from which to change, to begin something new. What then begins is the constant shifting and shuffling in utter sterility which are characteristic of many new nations that had the bad luck to be born in an age of propaganda.

That facts are not secure in the hands of power is obvious, but the point here is that power, by its very nature, can never produce a substitute for the secure stability of factual reality, which, because it is past, has grown into a dimension beyond our reach. Facts assert themselves by being stubborn, and their fragility is oddly combined with great resiliency—the same irreversibility that is the hallmark of all human action. In their stubbornness, facts are superior to power; they are less transitory than power formations, which arise when men get together for a purpose but disappear as soon as the purpose is either achieved or lost. This transitory character makes power a highly unreliable instrument for achieving permanence of any kind, and, therefore, not only truth and facts are insecure in its hands but untruth and non-facts as well. The political attitude toward facts must, indeed, tread the very narrow path between the danger of taking them as the results of some necessary development which men could not prevent and about which they can therefore do nothing and the danger of denying them, of trying to manipulate them out of the world.

V

In conclusion, I return to the questions I raised at the beginning of these reflections. Truth, though powerless and always defeated in a head-on clash with the powers that be, possesses a strength of its own: whatever those in power may contrive, they are unable to discover or invent a viable substitute for it. Persuasion and violence can destroy truth, but they cannot replace it. And this applies to rational or religious truth just as it applies, more obviously, to factual truth. To look upon politics from the perspective of truth, as I have done here, means to take one's stand outside the political realm. This standpoint is the standpoint of the truthteller, who forfeits his position—and, with it, the validity of what he has to say—if he tries to interfere directly in human affairs and to speak the language of persuasion or of violence. It is to this position and its significance for the political realm that we must now turn our attention.

The standpoint outside the political realm—outside the community to which we belong and the company of our peers—is clearly characterized as one of the various modes of being alone. Outstanding among the existential modes of truthtelling are the solitude of the philosopher, the isolation of the scientist and the artist, the impartiality of the historian and the judge, and the independence of the fact-finder, the witness, and the reporter. (This impartiality differs from that of the qualified, representative opinion, mentioned earlier, in that it is not acquired inside the political realm but is inherent in the position of the outsider required for such occupations.) These modes of being alone differ in many respects, but they have in common that as long as any one of them lasts, no political commitment, no adherence to a cause, is possible. They are, of course, common to all men; they are modes of human existence as such. Only when one of them is adopted as a way of life—and even then life is never lived in complete solitude or isolation or independence—is it likely to conflict with the demands of the political.

It is quite natural that we become aware of the nonpolitical and, potentially, even anti-political nature of truth—*Fiat veritas, et pereat mundus*—only in the event of conflict, and I have stressed up to now this side of the matter. But this cannot possibly tell the whole story. It leaves out of account certain public institutions, established and supported by the powers that be, in which, contrary to all political rules, truth and truthfulness have always constituted the highest criterion of speech and endeavor. Among these we find notably the judiciary, which either as a branch of government or as direct administration of justice is carefully protected against social and political power, as well as all institutions of higher learning, to which the state entrusts the education of its future citizens. To the extent that the Academe remembers its ancient origins, it must know that it was founded by the polis's most determined and most influential opponent. To be sure, Plato's dream did not come true: the Academe never became a counter-society, and nowhere do we hear of any attempt by the universities at seizing power. But what Plato never dreamed of did come true: The political realm recognized that it needed an institution outside the power struggle in addition to the impartiality required in the administration of justice; for whether these places of higher learning are in private or in public hands is of no great importance; not only their integrity but their very existence depends upon the good will of the government anyway. Very unwelcome truths have emerged from the universities, and very unwelcome judgments have been handed down from the bench time and again; and these institutions, like other refuges of truth, have remained exposed to all the dangers arising from social and political power. Yet the chances for truth to prevail in public are, of course, greatly improved by the mere existence of such places and by the organization of independent, supposedly disinterested scholars associated with them. And it can hardly be denied that, at least in constitutionally ruled countries, the political realm has recognized, even in the event of conflict, that it has a stake in the existence of men and institutions over which it has no power.

This authentically political significance of the Academe is today easily overlooked because of the prominence of its professional schools and the evolution of its natural-science divisions, where, unexpectedly, pure research has yielded so many decisive results that have proved vital to the country at large. No one can possibly gainsay the social and technical usefulness of the universities, but this importance is not political. The historical sciences and the humanities, which are supposed to find out, stand guard over, and interpret factual truth and human documents, are politically of greater relevance. The telling of factual truth comprehends much more than the daily information supplied by journalists, though without them we should never find our bearings in an ever-changing world and, in the most literal sense, would never know where we are. This is, of course, of the most immediate political importance; but if the press should ever really become the "fourth branch of government," it would have to be protected against government power and social pressure even more carefully than the judiciary is. For this very important political function of supplying information is exercised from outside the political realm, strictly speaking; no action and no decision are, or should be, involved.

Reality is different from, and more than, the totality of facts and events, which, anyhow, is unascertainable. Who says what is—λέγει τὰ ἐόντα—always tells a story, and in this story the particular facts lose their contingency and acquire some humanly comprehensible meaning. It is perfectly true that "all sorrows can be borne if you put them into a story or tell a story about them," in the words of Isak Dinesen, who not only was one of the great storytellers of our time but also—and she was almost unique in this respect—knew what she was doing. She could have added that joy and bliss, too, become bearable and meaningful for men only when they can talk about them and tell them as a story. To the extent that the teller of factual truth is also a storyteller, he brings about that "reconciliation with reality" which Hegel, the philosopher of history *par excellence*, understood as the ultimate goal of all philosophical thought, and which, indeed, has been the secret motor of all historiography that transcends mere learnedness. The transformation of the given raw material of sheer happenings which the historian, like the fiction writer (a good novel is by no means a simple concoction or a figment of pure fantasy), must effect is closely akin to the poet's transfiguration of moods or movements of the heart—the transfiguration of grief into lamentations or of jubilation into praise. We may see, with Aristotle, in the poet's political function the operation of a catharsis, a cleansing or purging of all emotions that could prevent men from acting. The political function of the story-teller—historian or novelist—is to teach acceptance of things as they are. Out of this acceptance, which can also be called truthfulness, arises the faculty of judgment—that, again in Isak Dinesen's words, "at the end we shall be privileged to view, and review, it—and that is what is named the day of judgment."

There is no doubt that all these politically relevant functions are performed from outside the political realm. They require non-commitment and impartiality, freedom from self-interest in thought and judgment. The disinterested pursuit of truth has a long history; its origin, characteristically, precedes all our theoretical and scientific traditions, including our tradition of philosophical and political thought. I think it can be traced to the moment when Homer chose to sing the deeds of the Trojans no less than those of the Achaeans, and to praise the glory of Hector, the foe and the defeated man, no less than the glory of Achilles, the hero of his kinfolk. This had happened nowhere before; no other civilization, however splendid, had been able to look with equal eyes upon friend and foe, upon success and defeat—which since Homer have not been recognized as ultimate standards of men's judgment, even though they are ultimates for the destinies of men's lives. Homeric impartiality echoes throughout Greek history, and it inspired the first great teller of factual truth, who became the father of history:

Herodotus tells us in the very first sentences of his stories that he set out to prevent "the great and wondrous deeds of the Greeks *and* the barbarians from losing their due meed of glory." This is the root of all so-called objectivity—this curious passion, unknown outside Western civilization, for intellectual integrity at any price. Without it no science would ever have come into being.

Since I have dealt here with politics from the perspective of truth, and hence from a viewpoint outside the political realm, I have failed to mention even in passing the greatness and the dignity of what goes on inside it. I have spoken as though the political realm were no more than a battlefield of partial, conflicting interests, where nothing counted but pleasure and profit, partisanship, and the lust for dominion. In short, I have dealt with politics as though I, too, believed that all public affairs were ruled by interest and power, that there would be no political realm at all if we were not bound to take care of life's necessities. The reason for this deformation is that factual truth clashes with the political only on this lowest level of human affairs, just as Plato's philosophical truth clashed with the political on the considerably higher level of opinion and agreement. From this perspective, we remain unaware of the actual content of political life—of the joy and the gratification that arise out of being in company with our peers, out of acting together and appearing in public, out of inserting ourselves into the world by word and deed, thus acquiring and sustaining our personal identity and beginning something entirely new. However, what I meant to show here is that this whole sphere, its greatness notwithstanding, is limited—that it does not encompass the whole of man's and the world's existence. It is limited by those things which men cannot change at will. And it is only by respecting its own borders that this realm, where we are free to act and to change, can remain intact, preserving its integrity and keeping its promises. Conceptually, we may call truth what we cannot change; metaphorically, it is the ground on which we stand and the sky that stretches above us.

Notes

1. *Eternal Peace*, Appendix I.
2. I quote from Spinoza's *Political Treatise* because it is noteworthy that even Spinoza, for whom the *libertas philosophandi* was the true end of government, should have taken so radical a position.
3. In the *Leviathan* (ch. 46) Hobbes explains that "disobedience may lawfully be punished in them, that against the laws teach even true philosophy." For is not "leisure the mother of philosophy; and Commonwealth the mother of peace and leisure"? And does it not follow that the Commonwealth will act in the interest of philosophy when it suppresses a truth which undermines peace? Hence the truthteller, in order to cooperate in an enterprise which is so necessary for his own peace of body and soul, decides to write what he knows "to be false philosophy." Of this Hobbes suspected Aristotle of all people, who according to him "writ it as a thing consonant to, and corroborative of [the Greeks'] religion: fearing the fate of Socrates." It never occurred to Hobbes that all search for truth would be self-defeating if its conditions could be guaranteed only by deliberate falsehoods. Then, indeed, everybody may turn out to be a liar like Hobbes' Aristotle. Unlike this figment of Hobbes'

logical fantasy, the real Aristotle was of course sensible enough to
leave Athens when he came to fear the fate of Socrates; he was not
wicked enough to write what he knew to be false, nor was he stupid
enough to solve his problem of survival by destroying everything
he stood for.

4. Ibid., ch. 11.

5. I hope no one will tell me any more that Plato was the inventor
of the "noble lie." This belief rested on a misreading of a crucial
passage (414C) in *The Republic*, where Plato speaks of one of his
myths—a "Phoenician tale"—as a ψεῦδος. Since the same Greek
word signifies "fiction," "error," and "lie" according to context—
when Plato wants to distinguish between error and lie, the Greek
language forces him to speak of "involuntary" and "voluntary"
ψεῦδος—the text can be rendered with Cornford as "bold flight
of invention" or be read with Eric Voegelin (*Order and History:
Plato and Aristotle*, Louisiana State University, 1957, vol. 3, p. 106)
as satirical in intention; under no circumstances can it be understood as a recommendation of lying as we understand it. Plato, of
course, was permissive about occasional lies to deceive the enemy
or insane people—*The Republic*, 382; they are "useful . . . in the way
of medicine . . . to be handled by no one but a physician," and the
physician of the polis is the ruler (388). But, contrary to the cave
allegory, no principle is involved in these passages.

6. *Leviathan*, Conclusion.

7. *The Federalist*, no. 49.

8. *Theologico-Political Treatise*, ch. 20.

9. See "What Is Enlightenment?" and "Was heisst sich im Denken
orientieren?"

10. *The Federalist*, no. 49.

11. *Timaeus*, 51D–52.

12. See *The Republic* 367. Compare also *Crito* 49 D: "For I know that
only a few men hold, or ever will hold, this opinion. Between those
who do and those who don't there can be no common deliberation;
they will necessarily look upon each other with contempt as to
their different purposes."

13. See *Gorgias* 482, where Socrates tells Callicles, his opponent, that
he will "not be in agreement with himself but that throughout
his life, he will contradict himself." He then adds: "I would much
rather that the whole world be not in agreement with me and talk

against me than that I, *who am one*, should be in discord with myself and talk in self-contradiction."

14. For a definition of thought as the silent dialogue between me and myself, see especially *Theaetetus* 189–190, and *Sophist* 263–264. It is quite in keeping with this tradition that Aristotle calls the friend, with whom you speak in the form of dialogue an αὐτὸς ἄλλος, another self.

15. *Nicomachean Ethics*, book 6, especially 1140b9 and 1141b4.

16. See Jefferson's "Draft Preamble to the Virginia Bill Establishing Religious Freedom."

17. This is the reason for Nietzsche's remark in "Schopenhauer als Erzieher": "Ich mache mir aus einem Philosophen gerade so viel, als er imstande ist, ein Beispiel zu geben."

18. In a letter to W. Smith, November 13, 1787.

19. *Critique of Judgment*, Paragraph 32.

20. Ibid., Paragraph 59.

21. For France, see the excellent article "'De Gaulle: Pose and Policy," in *Foreign Affairs*, July 1965. The Adenauer quotation is from his *Memoirs 1945–1953*, Chicago, 1966, p. 89, where, however, he puts this notion into the minds of the occupation authorities. But he has repeated the gist of it many times during his chancellorship.

22. Parts of the archive were published in Merle Fainsod, *Smolensk Under Soviet Rule*, Cambridge, Mass., 1958. See p. 374.

LYING IN POLITICS

Reflections on the Pentagon Papers

"The picture of the world's greatest superpower killing
or seriously injuring a thousand non-combatants a
week, while trying to pound a tiny backward nation
into submission on an issue whose merits are hotly
disputed, is not a pretty one."

—ROBERT S. MCNAMARA

I

THE PENTAGON PAPERS—as the forty-seven-volume
"History of U.S. Decision-Making Process on Vietnam Policy" (commissioned by Secretary of Defense Robert S. McNamara in June 1967 and completed a year and
a half later) has become known ever since the New York
Times published, in June 1971, this top-secret, richly documented record of the American role in Indochina from
World War II to May 1968—tell different stories, teach different lessons to different readers. Some claim they have
only now understood that Vietnam was the "logical" outcome of the Cold War or the anti-Communist ideology,
others that this is a unique opportunity to learn about
decision-making processes in government, but most

readers have by now agreed that the basic issue raised by the papers is deception. At any rate, it is quite obvious that this issue was uppermost in the minds of those who compiled *The Pentagon Papers* for the New York *Times*, and it is at least probable that this was also an issue for the team of writers who prepared the forty-seven volumes of the original study.[1] The famous credibility gap, which has been with us for six long years, has suddenly opened up into an abyss. The quicksand of lying statements of all sorts, deceptions as well as self-deceptions, is apt to engulf any reader who wishes to probe this material, which, unhappily, he must recognize as the infrastructure of nearly a decade of United States foreign and domestic policy.

Because of the extravagant lengths to which the commitment to nontruthfulness in politics went on at the highest level of government, and because of the concomitant extent to which lying was permitted to proliferate throughout the ranks of all governmental services, military and civilian—the phony body counts of the "search-and-destroy" missions, the doctored after-damage reports of the air force,[2] the "progress" reports to Washington from the field written by subordinates who knew that their performance would be evaluated by their own reports[3]—one is easily tempted to forget the background of past history, itself not exactly a story of immaculate virtue, against which this newest episode must be seen and judged.

Secrecy—what diplomatically is called "discretion," as well as the *arcana imperii*, the mysteries of government—and deception, the deliberate falsehood and the outright lie used as legitimate means to achieve political ends, have been with us since the beginning of recorded history. Truthfulness has never been counted among the political virtues, and lies have always been regarded as justifiable tools in political dealings. Whoever reflects on these matters can only be surprised by how little attention has been paid, in our tradition of philosophical and political thought, to their significance, on the one hand for the nature of action and, on the other, for the nature of our ability to deny in thought and word whatever happens to be the case. This active, aggressive capability is clearly different from our passive susceptibility to falling prey to error, illusion, the distortions of memory, and to whatever else can be blamed on the failings of our sensual and mental apparatus.

A characteristic of human action is that it always begins something new, and this does not mean that it is ever permitted to start *ab ovo*, to create *ex nihilo*. In order to make room for one's own action, something that was there before must be removed or destroyed, and things as they were before are changed. Such change would be impossible if we could not mentally remove ourselves from where we physically are located and *imagine* that things might as well be different from what they actually are. In other words, the deliberate denial of factual truth—the ability to lie—and the capacity to change facts—the ability to act—are interconnected; they owe their existence to the same source: imagination. It is by no means a matter of course that we can *say*, "The sun shines," when it actually is raining (the consequence of certain brain injuries is the loss of this capacity); rather, it indicates that while we are well equipped for the world, sensually as well as mentally, we are not fitted or embedded into it as one of its inalienable parts. We are *free* to change the world and to start something new in it. Without the mental freedom to deny or affirm existence, to say "yes" or "no"—not just to statements or propositions in order to express agreement or disagreement, but to things as they are given, beyond agreement or disagreement, to our organs of perception and cognition—no action would be possible; and action is of course the very stuff politics are made of.[4]

Hence, when we talk about lying, and especially about lying among acting men, let us remember that the lie did not creep into politics by some accident of human sinfulness. Moral outrage, for this reason alone, is not likely to make it disappear. The deliberate falsehood deals with *contingent* facts; that is, with matters that carry no inherent truth within themselves, no necessity to be as they are. Factual truths are never compellingly true. The historian knows how vulnerable is the whole texture of facts in which we spend our daily life; it is always in danger of being perforated by single lies or torn to shreds by the organized lying of groups, nations, or classes, or denied and distorted, often carefully covered up by reams of falsehoods or simply allowed to fall into oblivion. Facts need testimony to be remembered and trustworthy witnesses to be established in order to find a secure dwelling place in the domain of human affairs. From this, it follows that no factual statement can ever be beyond doubt—as secure and shielded against attack as, for instance, the statement that two and two make four.

It is this fragility that makes deception so very easy *up to a point*, and so tempting. It never comes into a conflict with reason, because things could indeed have been as the liar maintains they were. Lies are often much more plausible, more appealing to reason, than reality, since the liar has the great advantage of knowing beforehand what the audience wishes or expects to hear. He has prepared his story for public consumption with a careful eye to making it credible, whereas reality has the disconcerting habit of confronting us with the unexpected, for which we were not prepared.

Under normal circumstances the liar is defeated by reality, for which there is no substitute; no matter how large the tissue of falsehood that an experienced liar has to offer, it will never be large enough, even if he enlists the help of computers, to cover the immensity of factuality. The liar, who may get away with any number of single falsehoods, will find it impossible to get away with lying on principle. This is one of the lessons that could be learned from the totalitarian experiments and the totalitarian rulers' frightening confidence in the power of lying—in their ability, for instance, to rewrite history again and again to adapt the past to the "political line" of the present moment or to eliminate data that did not fit their ideology. Thus, in a socialist economy, they would deny that unemployment existed, the unemployed person simply becoming a non-person.

The results of such experiments when undertaken by those in possession of the means of violence are terrible enough, but lasting deception is not among them. There always comes the point beyond which lying becomes counterproductive. This point is reached when the audience to which the lies are addressed is forced to disregard altogether the distinguishing line between truth and falsehood in order to be able to survive. Truth or falsehood—it does not matter which any more, if your life depends on your acting as though you trusted; truth that can be relied on disappears entirely from public life, and with it the chief stabilizing factor in the ever-changing affairs of men.

To the many genres in the art of lying developed in the past, we must now add two more recent varieties. There is, *first*, the apparently innocuous one of the public-relations managers in government who learned their trade from the inventiveness of Madison Avenue. Public relations is but a variety of advertising; hence it has its origin in the consumer society, with its inordinate appetite for goods to be distributed through a market economy. The trouble with the mentality of the public-relations man is that he deals only in opinions and "good will," the readiness to buy, that is, in intangibles whose concrete reality is at a minimum. This means that for his inventions it may indeed look as though the sky is the limit, for he lacks the politician's power to act, to "create" facts, and, thus, that simple everyday reality that sets limits to power and brings the forces of imagination down to earth.

The only limitation to what the public-relations man does comes when he discovers that the same people who perhaps can be "manipulated" to buy a certain kind of soap cannot be manipulated—though, of course, they can be forced by terror—to "buy" opinions and political views. Therefore the psychological premise of human manipulability has become one of the chief wares that are sold on the market of common and learned opinion. But such doctrines do not change the way people form opinions or prevent them from acting according to their own lights. The only method short of terror to have real influence on their conduct is still the old carrot-and-stick approach. It is not surprising that the recent generation of intellectuals, who grew up in the insane atmosphere of rampant advertising and were taught that half of politics is "image-making" and the other half the art of making people believe in the imagery, should almost automatically fall back on the older adages of carrot and stick whenever the situation becomes too serious for "theory." To them, the greatest disappointment in the Vietnam adventure should have been the discovery that there are people with whom carrot-and-stick methods do not work either.

(Oddly enough, the only person likely to be an ideal victim of complete manipulation is the President of the United States. Because of the immensity of his job, he must surround himself with advisers, the "National Security Managers," as they have recently been called by Richard J. Barnet, who "exercise their power chiefly by filtering the information that reaches the President and by interpreting the outside world for him."[5] The President, one is tempted to argue, allegedly the most powerful man of the most powerful country, is the only person in this country whose range of choices can be predetermined. This, of course, can happen only if the executive branch has cut itself off from contact with the legislative powers of Congress; it is the logical outcome in our system of government when the Senate is being deprived of, or is reluctant to exercise, its powers to participate and advise in the conduct of foreign affairs. One of the Senate's functions, as we now know, is to shield the decision-making process against the transient moods and trends of society at large—in this case, the antics of our consumer society and the public-relations managers who cater to it.)

The *second* new variety of the art of lying, though less frequently met with in everyday life, plays a more important role in the Pentagon papers. It also appeals to much better men, to those, for example, who are likely to be found in the higher ranks of the civilian services. They are, in Neil Sheehan's felicitous phrase, professional "problem-solvers,"[6] and they were drawn into government from the universities and the various think tanks, some of them equipped with game theories and systems analyses, thus prepared, as they thought, to solve all the "problems" of foreign policy. A significant number of the authors of the McNamara study belong to this group, which consisted of eighteen military officers and eighteen civilians from think tanks, universities, and government services. They certainly "were not a flock of doves"—a mere "handful were critical of the U.S. commitment" in Vietnam[7]—and yet it is to them that we owe this truthful, though of course not complete, story of what happened inside the machinery of government.

The problem-solvers have been characterized as men of great self-confidence, who "seem rarely to doubt their ability to prevail," and they worked together with the members of the military of whom "the history remarks that they were 'men accustomed to winning.'"[8] We should not forget that we owe it to the problem-solvers' effort at impartial self-examination, rare among such people, that the actors' attempts at hiding their role behind a screen of self-protective secrecy (at least until they have completed their memoirs—in our century the most deceitful genre of literature) were frustrated. The basic integrity of those who wrote the report is beyond doubt; they could indeed be trusted by Secretary McNamara to produce an "encyclopedic and objective" report and "to let the chips fall where they may."[9]

But these moral qualities, which deserve admiration, clearly did not prevent them from participating for many years in the game of deceptions and falsehoods. Confident "of place, of education and accomplishment,"[10] they lied perhaps out of a mistaken patriotism. But the point is that they lied not so much for their country—certainly not for their country's survival, which was never at stake—as for its "image." In spite of their undoubted intelligence—it is manifest in many memos from their pens—they also believed that politics is but a variety of public relations, and they were taken in by all the bizarre psychological premises underlying this belief.

Still, they obviously were different from the ordinary image-makers. Their distinction lies in that they were problem-solvers as well. Hence they were not just intelligent, but prided themselves on being "rational," and they were indeed to a rather frightening degree above "sentimentality" and in love with "theory," the world of sheer mental effort. They were eager to find formulas, preferably expressed in a pseudo-mathematical language, that would unify the most disparate phenomena with which reality presented them; that is, they were eager to discover *laws* by which to explain and predict political and historical facts as though they were as necessary, and thus as reliable, as the physicists once believed natural phenomena to be.

However, unlike the natural scientist, who deals with matters that, whatever their origin, are not man-made or man-enacted, and that therefore can be observed, understood, and eventually even changed only through the most meticulous loyalty to factual, given reality, the historian, as well as the politician, deals with human affairs that owe their existence to man's capacity for action, and that means to man's relative freedom from things as they are. Men who act, to the extent that they feel themselves to be the masters of their own futures, will forever be tempted to make themselves masters of the past, too. Insofar as they have the appetite for action and are also in love with theories, they will hardly have the natural scientist's patience to wait until theories and hypothetical explanations are verified or denied by facts. Instead, they will be tempted to fit their reality—which, after all, was man-made to begin with and thus could have been otherwise—into their theory, thereby mentally getting rid of its disconcerting *contingency*.

Reason's aversion to contingency is very strong; it was Hegel, the father of grandiose history schemes, who held that "philosophical contemplation has no other intention than to eliminate the accidental."[11] Indeed, much of the modern arsenal of political theory—the game theories and systems analyses, the scenarios written for imagined "audiences," and the careful enumeration of, usually, three "options"—A, B, C—whereby A and C represent the opposite extremes and B the "logical" middle-of-the-road "solution" of the problem—has its source in this deep-seated aversion. The fallacy of such thinking begins with forcing the choices into mutually exclusive dilemmas; reality never presents us with anything so neat as premises for logical conclusions. The kind of thinking that presents both A and C as undesirable, therefore settles on B, hardly serves any other purpose than to divert the mind and blunt the judgment for the multitude of real possibilities. What these problem-solvers have in common with down-to-earth liars is the attempt to get rid of facts and the confidence that this should be possible because of the inherent contingency of facts.

The truth of the matter is that this can never be done by either theory or opinion manipulation—as though a fact is safely removed from the world if only enough people believe in its nonexistence. It can be done only through radical destruction—as in the case of the murderer who *says* that Mrs. Smith has died and then goes and kills her. In the political domain, such destruction would have to be wholesale. Needless to say, there never existed on any level of government such a will to wholesale destruction, in spite of the fearful number of war crimes committed in the course of the Vietnam war. But even where this will is present, as it was in the case of both Hitler and Stalin, the power to achieve it would have to amount to omnipotence. In order to eliminate Trotsky's role from the history of the Russian Revolution, it is not enough to kill him and eliminate his name from all Russian records so long as one cannot kill all his contemporaries and wield power over the libraries and archives of all countries of the earth.

II

That concealment, falsehood, and the role of the deliberate lie became the chief issues of the Pentagon papers, rather than illusion, error, miscalculation, and the like, is mainly due to the strange fact that the mistaken decisions and lying statements consistently violated the astoundingly accurate factual reports of the intelligence community, at least as recorded in the Bantam edition. The crucial point here is not merely that the policy of lying was hardly ever aimed at the enemy (this is one of the reasons why the papers do not reveal any military secrets that could fall under the Espionage Act), but was destined chiefly, if not exclusively, for domestic consumption, for propaganda at home, and especially for the purpose of deceiving Congress. The Tonkin incident, where the enemy knew all the facts and the Senate Foreign Relations Committee none, is a case in point.

Of even greater interest is that nearly all decisions in this disastrous enterprise were made in full cognizance of the fact that they probably could not be carried out: hence goals had constantly to be shifted. There are, first, the publicly proclaimed objectives—"seeing that the people of South Vietnam are permitted to determine their future" or "assisting the country to win their contest against the

. . . Communist conspiracy" or the containment of China and the avoidance of the domino effect or the protection of America's reputation "as a counter-subversive guarantor."[12] To these Dean Rusk has recently added the aim of preventing World War III, though it seems not to be in the Pentagon papers or to have played a role in the factual record as we know it. The same flexibility marks tactical considerations: North Vietnam is being bombed in order to prevent "a collapse of national morale"[13] in the South and, particularly, the breakdown of the Saigon government. But when the first raids were scheduled to start, the government had broken down, "pandemonium reigned in Saigon," the raids had to be postponed and a new goal found.[14] Now the objective was to compel "Hanoi to stop the Vietcong and the Pathet Lao," an aim that even the Joint Chiefs of Staff did not hope to attain. As they said, "it would be idle to conclude that these efforts will have a decisive effect."[15]

From 1965 on, the notion of a clear-cut victory receded into the background and the objective became "to convince the enemy that *he* could not win" (italics added). Since the enemy remained unconvinced, the next goal appeared: "to avoid a humiliating defeat"—as though the hallmark of a defeat in war were mere humiliation. What the Pentagon papers report is the haunting fear of the impact of defeat, not on the welfare of the nation, but "on the *reputation* of the United States and its President" (italics added). Thus, shortly before, during the many debates about the advisability of using ground troops against North Vietnam, the dominant argument was not fear of defeat itself and concern with the welfare of the troops in the case of withdrawal, but: "Once U.S. troops are in, it will be difficult to withdraw them . . . without *admitting* defeat" (italics added).[16] There was, finally, the "political" aim "to show the world the lengths to which the United States will go for a friend" and "to fulfill commitments."[17]

All these goals existed together, in an almost helter-skelter fashion; none was permitted to cancel its predecessors. Each addressed itself to a different "audience," and for each a different "scenario" had to be produced. John T. McNaughton's much-quoted enumeration of U.S. aims in 1965, "70%—To avoid a humiliating U.S. defeat (to our reputation as a guarantor). 20%—To keep SVN [South Vietnam] (and the adjacent) territory from Chinese hands. 10%—To permit the people of SVN to enjoy a better, freer way of life,"[18] is refreshing in its honesty, but was probably drawn up to bring some order and clarity into the debates on the forever troublesome question of why we were conducting a war in Vietnam, of all places. In a previous draft memorandum (1964), McNaughton had shown, perhaps unwittingly, how little he himself, even at that early stage of the bloody game, believed in the attainability of any substantial objectives: "Should South Vietnam disintegrate completely beneath us, we should try to hold it together long enough to permit us to try to evacuate our forces and *to convince the world* to accept the uniqueness (and congenital impossibility) of the South Vietnamese case" (italics added).[19]

"To convince the world"; to "demonstrate that U.S. was a 'good doctor' willing to keep promises, be tough, take risks, get bloodied and hurt the enemy badly";[20] to use a "tiny backward nation" devoid of any strategic importance "as a *test case* of U.S. capacity to help a nation meet a Communist 'war of liberation'" (italics added);[21] to keep intact an image of omnipotence, "our worldwide position of leadership";[22] to demonstrate "the will and the ability of the United States to have its way in world affairs";[23] to show "the credibility of our pledges to friends and allies";[24] in short, to "*behave* like" (italics added) the "greatest power in the world" for no other reason than to convince the world of this "simple fact" (in Walt Rostow's words)[25]—this was the only permanent goal that, with the beginning of the Johnson administration, pushed into the background all other goals and theories, the domino theory and anti-Communist strategy of the initial stages of the Cold War period as well as the counterinsurgency strategy so dear to the Kennedy administration.

The ultimate aim was neither power nor profit. Nor was it even influence in the world in order to serve particular, tangible interests for the sake of which prestige, an image of the "greatest power in the world," was needed and purposefully used. The goal was now the image itself, as is manifest in the very language of the problem-solvers, with their "scenarios" and "audiences," borrowed from the theater. For this ultimate aim, all policies became short-term interchangeable means, until finally, when all signs pointed to defeat in the war of attrition, the goal was no longer one of avoiding humiliating defeat but of finding ways and means to avoid admitting it and "save face."

Image-making as global policy—not world conquest, but victory in the battle "to win the people's minds"— is indeed something new in the huge arsenal of human follies recorded in history. This was not undertaken by a third-rate nation always apt to boast in order to compensate for the real thing, or by one of the old colonial powers that lost their position as a result of World War II and might have been tempted, as De Gaulle was, to bluff their way back to pre-eminence, but by "the dominant power" at the war's end. It may be natural for elected officeholders—who owe so much, or *believe* they owe so much, to their campaign managers—to think that manipulation is the ruler of the people's minds and hence the true ruler of the world. (The rumor, recently reported in the "Notes and Comment" section of *The New Yorker*, that "the Nixon-Agnew Administration was planning a campaign, organized and directed by Herb Klein, its director of communications, to destroy the 'credibility' of the press before the 1972 Presidential election" is quite in line with this public-relations mentality.)[26]

What is surprising is the eagerness of those scores of "intellectuals" who offered their enthusiastic help in this imaginary enterprise, perhaps because they were

fascinated by the sheer size of the mental exercises it
seemed to demand. Again, it may be only natural for
problem-solvers, trained in translating all factual contents into the language of numbers and percentages,
where they can be calculated, to remain unaware of the
untold misery that their "solutions"—pacification and
relocation programs, defoliation, napalm, and antiper-
sonnel bullets—held in store for a "friend" who needed
to be "saved" and for an "enemy" who had neither the will
nor the power to be one before we attacked him. But since
they dealt with the people's minds, it remains astonish-
ing that apparently none of them sensed that the "world"
might get rather frightened of American friendship and
commitment when the "lengths to which the U.S. will
go to fulfill" them were "shown" and contemplated.[27] No
reality and no common sense could penetrate the minds
of the problem-solvers[28] who indefatigably prepared their
scenarios for "relevant audiences" in order to change their
states of mind—"the Communists (who must feel strong
pressures), the South Vietnamese (whose morale must be
buoyed), our allies (who must trust us as 'underwriters')
and the U.S. public (which must support the risk-taking
with U.S. lives and prestige)."[29]

We know today to what extent all these audiences
were misjudged; according to Richard J. Barnet, in his
excellent contribution to the book *Washington Plans
an Aggressive War*, the "war became a disaster because
the National Security Managers misjudged each audi-

ence."[30] But the greatest, indeed basic, misjudgment was to address audiences with the means of war, to decide military matters from a "political and public-relations perspective" (whereby "political" meant the perspective of the next Presidential election and "public relations" the U.S. world image), and to think not about the real risks but of "techniques to minimize the impact of bad outcomes." Among proposals for the latter, the creation of "diversionary 'offensives' elsewhere in the world" was recommended, together with the launching of "an 'anti-poverty' program for underdeveloped areas."[31] Not for a moment did it occur to McNaughton, the author of this memorandum, who doubtless was an unusually intelligent man, that his diversions, unlike the diversions of the theater, would have had grave and totally unpredictable consequences; they would have changed the very world in which the U.S. moved and conducted its war.

It is this remoteness from reality that will haunt the reader of the Pentagon papers who has the patience to stay with them to the end. Barnet, in the essay mentioned above, has this to say on the matter: "The bureaucratic model had completely displaced reality: the hard and stubborn facts, which so many intelligence analysts were paid so much to collect, were ignored."[32] I am not sure that the evils of bureaucracy suffice as an explanation, though they certainly facilitated this defactualization. At any rate, the relation, or, rather, nonrelation, between facts and decision, between the intelligence community and the civilian and military services, is perhaps the most momentous, and certainly the best-guarded, secret that the Pentagon papers revealed.

It would be of great interest to know what enabled the intelligence services to remain so close to reality in this "Alice-in-Wonderland atmosphere," which the papers ascribe to the strange operations of the Saigon government but which seems in retrospect to more aptly describe the defactualized world where political goals were set and military decisions were made. For the beginnings of the role of the services in Southeast Asia were far from promising. Early in *The Pentagon Papers* we find recorded the decision to embark upon "covert warfare" in the early years of the Eisenhower administration, when the executive still believed it needed congressional authority to start a war. Eisenhower was still old-fashioned enough to believe in the Constitution. He met with congressional leaders and decided against open intervention because he was informed that Congress would not support such a decision.[33] When later, beginning with the Kennedy administration, "overt warfare," that is, the dispatching of "combat troops," was discussed, "the question of Congressional authority for open acts of war against a sovereign nation was never seriously raised."[34] Even when, under Johnson, foreign governments were thoroughly briefed on our plans for bombing North Vietnam, similar briefing of and consultation with congressional leaders seem never to have taken place.[35]

During Eisenhower's administration the Saigon Military Mission was formed, under the command of Colonel Edward Lansdale, and told "to undertake paramilitary operations . . . and to wage political-psychological warfare."[36] This meant in practice to print leaflets that would spread lies falsely attributed to the other side, to pour "contaminant in the engines" of the bus company of Hanoi before the French left the North, to conduct an "English-language class . . . for mistresses of important personages," and to hire a team of Vietnamese astrologers.[37] This ludicrous phase continued into the early sixties, until the military took over. After the Kennedy administration, the counterinsurgency doctrine receded into the background—perhaps because, during the overthrow of President Ngo Dinh Diem, it turned out that the C.I.A.-financed Vietnamese Special Forces "had in effect become the private army of Mr. Nhu," Diem's brother and political adviser.[38]

The fact-finding branches of the intelligence services were separated from whatever covert operations were still going on in the field, which meant that they at least were responsible only for gathering information, rather than for creating the news themselves. They had no need to show positive results and were under no pressure from Washington to produce good news to feed into the public-relations machine, or to concoct fairy tales about "continuing progress, virtually miraculous improvement, year in and year out."[39] They were relatively independent, and the result was that they told the truth, year in and year out. It seems that in these intelligence services people did not tell "their superiors what they thought they wanted to hear," that "assessments were [not] made by the imple-menters," and that no commanding officer told his agents what "an American division commander told one of his district advisers, who insisted on reporting the persistent presence of unpacified Vietcong hamlets in his area: 'Son, you're writing our own report card in this country. Why are you failing us?'"[40] It also seems that those who were responsible for intelligence estimates were miles away from the problem-solvers, their disdain for facts, and the accidental character of all facts. The price they paid for these objective advantages was that their reports remained without any influence on the decisions and propositions of the National Security Council.

After 1963, the only discernible trace of the covert-war period is the infamous "provocation strategy," that is, a whole program of "deliberate attempts to provoke the D.R.V. [Democratic Republic of (North) Vietnam] into taking actions which could then be answered by a sys-tematic U.S. air campaign."[41] These tactics do not belong among the ruses of war. They have been typical of the secret police and became notorious as well as counterpro-ductive in the declining days of czarist Russia, when the agents of the Okhrana, by organizing spectacular assas-sinations, "served despite themselves the ideas of those whom they denounced."[42]

III

The divergence between facts—established by the intelligence services, sometimes by the decision-makers themselves (as notably in the case of McNamara), and often available to the informed public—and the premises, theories, and hypotheses according to which decisions were finally made is total. And the extent of our failures and disasters throughout these years can be grasped only if one has the totality of this divergence firmly in mind. I shall therefore remind the reader of a few outstanding examples.

As regards the domino theory, first enunciated in 1950[43] and permitted to survive, as has been said, the "most momentous events": To the question of President Johnson in 1964, "Would the rest of Southeast Asia necessarily fall if Laos and South Vietnam came under North Vietnamese control?" the C.I.A.'s answer was, "With the possible exception of Cambodia, it is likely that no nation in the area would quickly succumb to Communism as a result of the fall of Laos and South Vietnam."[44] When five years later the Nixon administration raised the same question, it "was advised by the Central Intelligence Agency . . . that [the United States] could immediately withdraw from South Vietnam and 'all of Southeast Asia would remain just as it is for at least another generation.'"[45] According to the Pentagon papers, "only the Joint Chiefs, Mr. [Walt W.] Rostow and General [Maxwell] Taylor appear to have accepted the domino theory in its literal sense,"[46] and the point here is that those who did not accept it still used it, not merely for public statements, but as part of their own premises as well.

As to the claim that the insurgents in South Vietnam were "externally directed and supported" by a "Communist conspiracy": The assessment of the intelligence community in 1961 was "that 80–90 per cent of the estimated 17,000 VC had been locally recruited, and that there was little evidence that the VC relied on external supplies."[47] Three years later the situation was unchanged: According to an intelligence analysis of 1964, "the primary sources of Communist strength in South Vietnam are indigenous."[48] In other words, the elementary fact of civil war in South Vietnam was not unknown in the circles of the decision-makers. Had not Senator Mike Mansfield warned Kennedy as early as 1962 that sending more military reinforcements to South Vietnam would mean that "the Americans would be dominating the combat in a civil war . . . [which] would hurt American prestige in Asia and would not help the South Vietnamese to stand on their own two feet, either"?[49]

The bombing of North Vietnam nevertheless was begun partly because theory said that "a revolution could be dried up by cutting off external sources of support and supply." The bombings were supposed to "break the will" of North Vietnam to support the rebels in the South, although the decision-makers themselves (in this case

McNaughton) knew enough of the indigenous nature of the revolt to doubt that the Viet Cong would "obey a caving" North Vietnam,[50] while the Joint Chiefs did not believe "that these efforts will have a decisive effect" on Hanoi's will to begin with.[51] In 1965, according to a report by McNamara, members of the National Security Council had agreed that North Vietnam "was not likely to quit . . . and in any case, they were more likely to give up because of VC failure in the South than because of bomb-induced 'pain' in the North."[52]

Finally there were, secondary only to the domino theory, the grand stratagems based on the premise of a monolithic Communist world conspiracy and the existence of a Sino-Soviet bloc, in addition to the hypothesis of Chinese expansionism. The notion that China must be "contained" has now, in 1971, been refuted by President Nixon; but more than four years ago McNamara wrote: "To the extent that our original intervention and our existing actions in Vietnam were motivated by the perceived need to draw the line against Chinese expansionism in Asia, our objective has already been attained,"[53] although, only two years earlier, he had agreed that the United States's aim in South Vietnam was "not to 'help friend' but to contain China."[54]

The war critics have denounced all these theories because of their obvious clash with known facts—such as the nonexistence of a Sino-Soviet bloc, known to everybody familiar with the history of the Chinese revolution and Stalin's resolute opposition to it, or the fragmented character of the Communist movement since the end of World War II. A number of these critics went further and developed a theory of their own: America, having emerged as the greatest power after World War II, has embarked upon a consistent imperialist policy that aims ultimately at world rule. The advantage of this theory was that it could explain the absence of national interest in the whole enterprise—the sign of imperialist aims having always been that they were neither guided nor limited by national interest and territorial boundaries—though it could hardly account for the fact that this country was madly insisting on "pouring its resources down the drain in the wrong place" (as George Ball, Under Secretary of State in the Johnson administration and the only adviser who dared to break the taboo and recommend immediate withdrawal, had the courage to tell the President in 1965).[55]

Clearly this was no case of "limited means to achieve excessive ends."[56] Was it excessive for a "superpower" to add one more small country to its string of client states or to win a victory over a "tiny backward nation"? It was, rather, an unbelievable example of using excessive means to achieve minor aims in a region of marginal interest. It was precisely this unavoidable impression of wrong-headed floundering that finally brought the country to the conviction "widely and strongly held that 'the Establishment' is out of its mind. The feeling is that we are trying to impose some U.S. image on distant peoples we cannot understand . . . and we are carrying the thing to absurd lengths," as McNaughton wrote in 1967.[57]

At any rate, the Bantam edition of the Pentagon papers contains nothing to support the theory of grandiose imperialist stratagems. Only twice is the importance of land, sea, and air bases, so decisively important for imperialist strategy, mentioned—once by the Joint Chiefs of Staff, who point out that "our ability in limited war" would be "markedly" reduced if a "loss of the Southeast Asian Mainland" resulted in the loss of "air, land and sea bases,"[58] and once in the McNamara report of 1964, which says explicitly: "We do *not* require that it [South Vietnam] serve as a Western base or as a member of a Western Alliance" (italics added).[59] The only public statements of the American government during this period that indeed told almost gospel truth were the often-repeated claims, ever so much less plausible than other public-relations notions, that we were seeking no territorial gains or any other tangible profit.

This is not to say that a genuine American global policy with imperialist overtones would have been impossible after the collapse of the old colonial powers. The Pentagon papers, generally so devoid of spectacular news, reveal one incident, never more than a rumor, so far as I know, that seems to indicate how considerable were the chances for a global policy that was then gambled away in the cause of image-making and winning people's minds. According to a cable from an American diplomat in Hanoi, Ho Chi Minh wrote several letters in 1945 and 1946 to President Truman requesting the United States "to support the idea of Annamese independence according to the *Philippines example*, to examine the case of the Annamese, and to take steps necessary to maintenance of world peace which is being endangered by French efforts to reconquer Indochina" (italics added).[60] It is true; similar letters were addressed to other countries, China, Russia, and Great Britain, none of which, however, at that particular moment would have been able to give the protection that was requested and that would have established Indochina in the same semiautonomous position as other client states of this country. A second and equally striking incident, apparently mentioned at the time by the Washington *Post*, was recorded in the "Special China Series," documents issued by the State Department in August, 1969, but came to the notice of the public only when reported by Terence Smith in the New York *Times*. Mao and Chou En-lai, it turns out, approached President Roosevelt in January, 1945, "trying to establish relations with the United States in order *to avoid total dependence on the Soviet Union*" (italics added). It seems that Ho Chi Minh never received an answer, and information of the Chinese approach was suppressed because, as Professor Allen Whiting has commented, it contradicted "the image of monolithic Communism directed from Moscow."[61]

Although the decision-makers certainly knew about

the intelligence reports, whose factual statements they had, as it were, to eliminate from their minds day in and day out, I think it entirely possible that they were not aware of these earlier documents, which would have given the lie to all their premises before they could grow into full-blown theory and ruin the country. Certain bizarre circumstances attending the recent irregular and unexpected declassification of top-secret documents point in this direction. It is astounding that the Pentagon papers could have been prepared over years while people in the White House, in the Department of State, and in the Defense Department apparently ignored the study; but it is even more astounding that after its completion, with sets dispatched in all directions within the government bureaucracy, the White House and the State Department were unable even to locate the forty-seven volumes, clearly indicating that those who should have been most concerned with what the study had to tell never set eyes on it.

This sheds some light on one of the gravest dangers of overclassification: not only are the people and their elected representatives denied access to what they must know to form an opinion and make decisions, but also the actors themselves, who receive top clearance to learn all the relevant facts, remain blissfully unaware of them. And this is so not because some invisible hand deliberately leads them astray, but because they work under circumstances, and with habits of mind, that allow them neither time nor inclination to go hunting for pertinent facts in mountains of documents, 99½ per cent of which should not be classified and most of which are irrelevant for all practical purposes. Even now that the press has brought a certain portion of this classified material into the public domain and members of Congress have been given the whole study, it does not look as though those most in need of this information have read it or ever will. At any event, the fact of the matter is that aside from the compilers themselves, "the people who read these documents in the *Times* were the first to study them,"[62] which makes one wonder about the cherished notion that government needs the *arcana imperii* to be able to function properly.

If the mysteries of government have so befogged the minds of the actors themselves that they no longer know or remember the truth behind their concealments and their lies, the whole operation of deception, no matter how well organized its "marathon information campaigns," in Dean Rusk's words, and how sophisticated its Madison Avenue gimmickry, will run aground or become counterproductive, that is, confuse people without convincing them. For the trouble with lying and deceiving is that their efficiency depends entirely upon a clear notion of the truth that the liar and deceiver wishes to hide. In this sense, truth, even if it does not prevail in public, possesses an ineradicable primacy over all falsehoods.

In the case of the Vietnam war we are confronted with, in addition to falsehoods and confusion, a truly amazing and entirely honest ignorance of the historically pertinent background: not only did the decision-makers seem ignorant of all the well-known facts of the Chinese revolution and the decade-old rift between Moscow and Peking that preceded it, but "no one at the top knew or considered it important that the Vietnamese had been fighting foreign invaders for almost 2,000 years,"[63] or that the notion of Vietnam as a "tiny backward nation" without interest to "civilized" nations, which is, unhappily, often shared by the war critics, stands in flagrant contradiction to the very old and highly developed culture of the region. What Vietnam lacks is not "culture," but strategic importance (Indochina is "devoid of decisive military objectives," as a Joint Chiefs of Staff memo said in 1954),[64] a suitable terrain for modern mechanized armies, and rewarding targets for the air force. What caused the disastrous defeat of American policies and armed intervention was indeed no quagmire ("the policy of 'one more step'—each new step always promising the success which the previous *last step* had also *promised* but had unaccountably failed to deliver," in the words of Arthur Schlesinger, Jr., as quoted by Daniel Ellsberg, who rightly denounces the notion as a "myth"),[65] but the willful, deliberate disregard of all facts, historical, political, geographical, for more than twenty-five years.

IV

If the quagmire model is a myth and if no grand imperialist stratagems or will to world conquest can be discovered, let alone interest in territorial gains, desire for profit,
or, least of all, concern about national security; if, moreover, the reader is disinclined to be satisfied with such
general notions as "Greek tragedy" (proposed by Max
Frankel and Leslie H. Gelb) or stab-in-the-back legends,
always dear to warmongers in defeat, then the question
recently raised by Ellsberg, *"How could they?"*[66]—rather
than deception and lying per se—will become the basic
issue of this dismal story. For the truth, after all, is that
the United States was the richest country and the dominant power after the end of World War II, and that today,
a mere quarter of a century later, Mr. Nixon's metaphor
of the "pitiful, helpless giant" is an uncomfortably apt
description of "the mightiest country on earth."

Unable to defeat, with a "1000-to-1 superiority in fire
power,"[67] a small nation in six years of overt warfare,
unable to take care of its domestic problems and halt the
swift decline of its large cities, having wasted its resources
to the point where inflation and currency devaluation
threaten its international trade as well as its standard of
life at home, the country is in danger of losing much more
than its claim to world leadership. And even if one antici-
pates the judgment of future historians who might see this
development in the context of twentieth-century history,

when the defeated nations in two world wars managed to come out on top in competition with the victors (chiefly because they were compelled by the victors to rid themselves for a relatively long period of the incredible wastefulness of armaments and military expenses), it remains hard to reconcile oneself to so much effort wasted on demonstrating the impotence of bigness—though one may welcome this unexpected, grand-scale revival of David's triumph over Goliath.

The first explanation that comes to mind to answer the question "How could they?" is likely to point to the interconnectedness of deception and self-deception. In the contest between public statements, always over-optimistic, and the truthful reports of the intelligence community, persistently bleak and ominous, the public statements were liable to win simply because they were public. The great advantage of publicly established and accepted propositions over whatever an individual might secretly know or believe to be the truth is neatly illustrated by a medieval anecdote according to which a sentry, on duty to watch and warn the townspeople of the enemy's approach, jokingly sounded a false alarm—and then was the last to rush to the walls to defend the town against his invented enemies. From this, one may conclude that the more successful a liar is, the more people he has convinced, the more likely it is that he will end by believing his own lies.

In the Pentagon papers we are confronted with people

who did their utmost to win the minds of the people, that is, to manipulate them; but since they labored in a free country, where all kinds of information were available, they never really succeeded. Because of their relatively high station and their position in government, they were better shielded—in spite of their privileged knowledge of "top secrets"—against this public information, which also more or less told the factual truth, than were those whom they tried to convince and of whom they were likely to think in terms of mere audiences, "silent majorities," who were supposed to watch the scenarists' productions. The fact that the Pentagon papers revealed hardly any spectacular news testifies to the liars' failure to create a convinced audience that they could then join themselves.

Still, the presence of what Ellsberg has called the process of "internal self-deception"[68] is beyond doubt, but it is as though the normal process of self-deceiving were reversed; it was not as though deception ended with self-deception. The deceivers started with self-deception. Probably because of their high station and their astounding self-assurance, they were so convinced of overwhelming success, not on the battlefield, but in the public-relations arena, and so certain of the soundness of their psychological premises about the unlimited possibilities in manipulating people, that they *anticipated* general belief and victory in the battle for people's minds. And since they lived in a defactualized world anyway, they did not find it difficult to pay no more attention to the fact that their audience refused to be convinced than to other facts.

The internal world of government, with its bureaucracy on one hand, its social life on the other, made self-deception relatively easy. No ivory tower of the scholars has ever better prepared the mind for ignoring the facts of life than did the various think tanks for the problem-solvers and the reputation of the White House for the President's advisers. It was in this atmosphere, where defeat was less feared than admitting defeat, that the misleading statements about the disasters of the Tet offensive and the Cambodian invasion were concocted. But what is even more important is that the truth about such decisive matters could be successfully covered up in these internal circles—but nowhere else—by worries about how to avoid becoming "the first American President to lose a war" and by the always present preoccupations with the next election.

So far as problem-solving, in contrast to public-relations managing, is concerned, self-deception, even "internal self-deception," is no satisfactory answer to the question "How could they?" Self-deception still presupposes a distinction between truth and falsehood, between fact and fantasy, and therefore a conflict between the real world and the self-deceived deceiver that disappears in an entirely defactualized world; Washington and its sprawling governmental bureaucracy, as well as the various think tanks in the country, provide the problem-solvers with a natural habitat for mind and body. In the realm of politics, where secrecy and deliberate deception have always played a significant role, self-deception is the danger par excellence; the self-deceived deceiver loses all contact with not only his audience, but also the real world, which still will catch up with him, because he can remove his mind from it but not his body. The problem-solvers who knew all the facts regularly presented to them in the reports of the intelligence community had only to rely on their shared techniques, that is, on the various ways of translating qualities and contents into quantities and numbers with which to calculate outcomes—which then, unaccountably, never came true—in order to eliminate, day in and day out, what they knew to be real. The reason this could work for so many years is precisely that "the goals pursued by the United States government were almost exclusively psychological,"[69] that is, matters of the mind.

Reading the memos, the options, the scenarios, the way percentages are ascribed to the potential risks and returns—"too many risks with too little return"[70]—of contemplated actions, one sometimes has the impression that a computer, rather than "decision-makers," had been let loose in Southeast Asia. The problem-solvers did not *judge*; they calculated. Their self-confidence did not even need self-deception to be sustained in the midst of so many misjudgments, for it relied on the evidence of mathematical, purely rational truth. Except, of course, that this "truth" was entirely irrelevant to the "problem" at hand. If, for instance, it can be calculated that the outcome of a certain action is "less likely to be a general war than more likely,"[71] it does not follow that we can choose it even if the proportion were eighty to twenty, because of the enormity and *incalculable quality* of the risk; and the same is true when the odds of reform in the Saigon government versus the "chance that we would wind up like the French in 1954" are 70 per cent to 30 per cent.[72] That is a nice outlook for a gambler, not for a statesman,[73] and even the gambler would be better advised to take into account what gain or loss would actually mean for him in daily life. Loss may mean utter ruin and gain no more than some welcome but nonessential improvement of his financial affairs. Only if nothing real is at stake for the gambler—a bit more or less money is not likely to make any difference in his standard of life—can he safely rely on the percentage game. The trouble with our conduct of the war in South Vietnam was that no such control, given by reality itself, ever existed in the minds of either the decision-makers or the problem-solvers.

It is indeed true that American policy pursued no real aims, good or bad, that could limit and control sheer fantasy: "Neither territory nor economic advantage has been pursued in Vietnam. The entire purpose of the enormous and costly effect has been to create a specific state of mind."[74] And the reason such excessively costly means, costly in human lives and material resources, were permitted to be used for such politically irrelevant ends must be sought not merely in the unfortunate superabundance in this country, but in its inability to understand that even great power is *limited* power. Behind the constantly repeated cliché of the "mightiest power on earth," there lurked the dangerous myth of omnipotence.

Just as Eisenhower was the last President who knew he would have to request "Congressional authority to commit American troops in Indochina," so his administration was the last to be aware that "the allocation of more than token U.S. armed forces in that area would be a serious diversion of *limited* U.S. capabilities" (italics added).[75] In spite of all the later calculations of "costs, returns and risks" of certain acts, the calculators remained totally unaware of any absolute, nonpsychological limitation. The limits they perceived were the people's minds, how much they would stand in the loss of American lives, which should not be much larger than, for instance, the loss in traffic accidents. But it apparently never occurred to them that there are limits to the resources that even this country can waste without going bankrupt.

This deadly combination of the "arrogance of power"— the pursuit of a mere image of omnipotence, as distinguished from an aim of world conquest, to be attained by nonexistent unlimited resources—with the arrogance of mind, an utterly irrational confidence in the calculability of reality, becomes the leitmotif of the decision-making processes from the beginning of escalation in 1964. This, however, is not to say that the problem-solvers' rigorous methods of defactualization are at the root of this relentless march into self-destruction.

The problem-solvers, who lost their minds because they trusted the calculating powers of their brains at the expense of the mind's capacity for experience and its ability to learn from it, were preceded by the ideologists of the Cold War period. Anti-Communism—not the old, often prejudiced hostility of America against socialism and communism, so strong in the twenties and still a mainstay of the Republican party during the Roosevelt administration, but the postwar comprehensive ideology—was originally the brain child of former Communists who needed a new ideology by which to explain and reliably foretell the course of history. This ideology was at the root of all "theories" in Washington since the end of World War II. I have mentioned the extent to which sheer ignorance of all pertinent facts and deliberate neglect of postwar developments became the hallmark of established doctrine within the establishment. They needed no facts, no information; they had a "theory," and all data that did not fit were denied or ignored.

The methods of this older generation—the methods of Mr. Rusk as distinguished from those of Mr. McNamara—were less complicated, less brainy, as it were, than those of the problem-solvers, but not less efficacious in shielding men from the impact of reality and in ruining the mind's capacity for judgment and for learning.

These men prided themselves on having learned from the past—from Stalin's rule over all Communist parties, hence the notion of "monolithic Communism," and from Hitler's starting a world war after Munich, from which they concluded that every gesture of reconciliation was a "second Munich." They were unable to confront reality on its own terms because they had always some parallels in mind that "helped" them to understand those terms. When Johnson, still in his capacity as Kennedy's Vice-President, came home from an inspection tour in South Vietnam and happily reported that Diem was the "Churchill of Asia," one would have thought that the parallelism game would die from sheer absurdity, but this was not the case. Nor can one say that the left-wing war critics thought in different terms. The extreme fringe had the unhappy inclination of denouncing as "fascist" or "nazi" whatever, often quite rightly, displeased them, and of calling every massacre a genocide, which obviously it was not; this could only help to produce a mentality that was quite willing to condone massacre and other war crimes so long as they were not genocide.

The problem-solvers were remarkably free from the sins of the ideologists; they believed in methods but not in "world views," which, incidentally, is the reason they could be trusted "to pull together the Pentagon's documentary record of the American involvement"[76] in a way that would be both "encyclopedic and objective."[77] But though they did not believe in such generally accepted

rationales for policies as the domino theory, these rationales, with their different methods of defactualization,
provided the atmosphere and the background against
which the problem-solvers then went to work; they had,
after all, to convince the cold warriors, whose minds then
turned out to be singularly well prepared for the abstract
games they had to offer.

How the cold warriors proceeded when left to themselves is well illustrated by one of the "theories" of Walt
Rostow, the Johnson administration's "dominant intellectual." It was Rostow's "theory" that became one of the
chief rationales for the decision to bomb North Vietnam
against the advice of "McNamara's then prestigious systems analysts in the Defense Department." His theory
seemed to have relied on the view of Bernard Fall, one
of the most acute observers and best-informed war critics, who had suggested that "Ho Chi Minh *might* disavow
the war in the South if some of his new industrial plants
were made a target"[78] (italics added). This was a hypothesis, a real possibility, which had to be either confirmed
or refuted. But the remark had the ill luck to fit well with
Rostow's theories about guerrilla warfare, and was now
transformed into a "fact": President Ho Chi Minh "has an
industrial complex to protect; he is no longer a guerrilla
fighter with nothing to lose."[79] This looks in retrospect,
in the eyes of the analyst, like a "colossal misjudgment."[80]
But the point is that the "misjudgment" could become
"colossal" only because no one wished to correct it in

time. It turned out very quickly that the country was not industrialized enough to suffer from air attacks in a *limited* war whose objective, changing over the years, was never the destruction of the enemy, but, characteristically, "to break his will"; and the government's will in Hanoi, whether or not the North Vietnamese possessed what in Rostow's view was a necessary quality of the guerrilla fighter, refused to be "broken."

To be sure, this failure to distinguish between a plausible hypothesis and the fact that must confirm it, that is, this dealing with hypotheses and mere "theories" as though they were established facts, which became endemic in the psychological and social sciences during the period in question, lacks all the rigor of the methods used by the game theorists and systems analysts. But the source of both—namely, the inability or unwillingness to consult experience and to learn from reality—is the same.

This brings us to the root of the matter that, at least partially, might contain the answer to the question, How could they not only start these policies but carry them through to their bitter and absurd end? Defactualization and problem-solving were welcomed because disregard of reality was inherent in the policies and goals themselves. What did they have to know about Indochina as it really was, when it was no more than a "test case" or a domino, or a means to "contain China" or prove that we *are* the mightiest of the superpowers? Or take the case of bombing North Vietnam for the ulterior purpose of building morale in South Vietnam,[81] without much intention of winning a clear-cut victory and ending the war. How could they be interested in anything as real as victory when they kept the war going not for territorial gain or economic advantage, least of all to help a friend or keep a commitment, and not even for the reality, as distinguished from the image, of power?

When this stage of the game was reached, the initial premise that we should never mind the region or the country itself—inherent in the domino theory—changed into "never mind the enemy." And this in the midst of a war! The result was that the enemy, poor, abused, and suffering, grew stronger while "the mightiest country" grew weaker with each passing year. There are historians today who maintain that Truman dropped the bomb on Hiroshima in order to scare the Russians out of Eastern Europe (with the result we know). If this is true, as it might well be, then we may trace back the earliest beginnings of the disregard for the actual consequences of action in favor of some ulterior calculated aim to the fateful war crime that ended the last world war. The Truman Doctrine, at any rate, "depicted a world full of dominoes," as Leslie H. Gelb has pointed out.

V

At the beginning of this analysis I tried to suggest that the aspects of the Pentagon papers that I have chosen, the aspects of deception, self-deception, image-making, ideologizing, and defactualization, are by no means the only features of the papers that deserve to be studied and learned from. There is, for instance, the fact that this massive and systematic effort at self-examination was commissioned by one of the chief actors, that thirty-six men could be found to compile the documents and write their analysis, quite a few of whom "had helped to develop or to carry out the policies they were asked to evaluate,"[82] that one of the authors, when it had become apparent that no one in government was willing to use or even to read the results, went to the public and leaked it to the press, and that, finally, the most respectable newspapers in the country dared to bring material that was stamped "top secret" to the widest possible attention. It has rightly been said by Neil Sheehan that Robert McNamara's decision to find out what went wrong, and why, "may turn out to be one of the most important decisions in his seven years at the Pentagon."[83] It certainly restored, at least for a fleeting moment, this country's reputation in the world. What had happened could indeed hardly have happened anywhere else. It is as though all these people, involved in an unjust war and rightly compromised by it, had suddenly remembered what they owed to their forefathers' "decent respect for the opinions of mankind."

What calls for further close and detailed study is the fact, much commented on, that the Pentagon papers revealed little significant news that was not available to the average reader of dailies and weeklies; nor are there any arguments, pro or con, in the "History of U.S. Decision-Making Process on Vietnam Policy" that have not been debated publicly for years in magazines, television shows, and radio broadcasts. (Personal positions and changes in them aside, the different views of the intelligence community on basic issues were the only matter generally unknown.) That the public had access for years to material that the government vainly tried to keep from it testifies to the integrity and to the power of the press even more forcefully than the way the *Times* broke the story. What has often been suggested has now been established: so long as the press is free and not corrupt, it has an enormously important function to fulfill and can rightly be called the fourth branch of government. Whether the First Amendment will suffice to protect this most essential political freedom, the right to unmanipulated factual information without which all freedom of opinion becomes a cruel hoax, is another question.

There is, finally, a lesson to be learned by those who, like myself, believed that this country had embarked on an imperialist policy, had utterly forgotten its old anticolonial sentiments, and was perhaps succeeding in establishing that Pax Americana that President Kennedy had denounced. Whatever the merits of these suspicions, and they could be justified by our policies in Latin America, if undeclared small wars—aggressive brush-fire operations in foreign lands—are among the necessary means to attain imperialist ends, the United States will be less able to employ them successfully than almost any other great power. For while the demoralization of American troops has by now reached unprecedented proportions— according to *Der Spiegel*, during the past year 89,088 deserters, 100,000 conscientious objectors, and tens of thousands of drug addicts[84]—the disintegration process of the army started much earlier and was preceded by similar developments during the Korean War.[85] One has only to talk to a few of the veterans of this war—or to read Daniel Lang's sober and telling report in *The New Yorker*[86] about the development of a fairly typical case—to realize that in order for this country to carry adventurous and aggressive policies to success there would have to be a decisive change in the American people's "national character." The same could of course be concluded from the extraordinarily strong, highly qualified, and well-organized opposition that has from time to time arisen at home. The North Vietnamese who watched these developments carefully over the years had their hopes always set on them, and it seems that they were right in their assessment.

No doubt all this can change. But one thing has become clear in recent months: the halfhearted attempts of the government to circumvent Constitutional guarantees and to intimidate those who have made up their minds not to be intimidated, who would rather go to jail than see their liberties nibbled away, are not enough and probably will not be enough to destroy the Republic. There is reason to hope, with Mr. Lang's veteran—one of the nation's two and a half million—"that the country might regain its better side as a result of the war. 'I know it's nothing to bet on,' he said, 'but neither is anything else I can think of.'"[87]

Notes

1. In the words of Leslie H. Gelb, who was in charge of the team: "Uppermost, of course, is the crucial question of governmental credibility." See "Today's Lessons from the Pentagon Papers," in *Life*, September 17, 1971.

2. Ralph Stavins, Richard J. Barnet, and Marcus G. Raskin, *Washington Plans an Aggressive War*, New York, 1971, pp. 185–187.

3. Daniel Ellsberg, "The Quagmire Myth and the Stalemate Machine," in *Public Policy*, Spring 1971, pp. 262–263. See also Leslie H. Gelb, "Vietnam: The System Worked," in *Foreign Policy*, Summer 1971, p. 153.

4. For more general considerations of the relation between truth and politics see my "Truth and Politics" in *Between Past and Future*, Second Edition, New York, 1968.

5. In Stavins, Barnet, Raskin, *op. cit.*, p. 199.

6. *The Pentagon Papers*, as published by the New York *Times*, New York, 1971, p. xiv. My essay was prepared before the appearance of the editions published by the Government Printing Office and Beacon Press, and therefore is based only on the Bantam edition.

7. Leslie H. Gelb, *op. cit.* in *Life*.

8. *The Pentagon Papers*, p. xiv.

9. Leslie H. Gelb, in *Life*.

10. *The Pentagon Papers*, p. xiv.

11. *Die Philosophische Weltgeschichte, Entwurf von 1830*: "Die philosophische Betrachtung hat keine andere Absicht als das Zufällige zu entfernen."

12. *The Pentagon Papers*, p. 190.

13. *Ibidem*, p. 312.

14. *Ibidem*, p. 392.

15. *Ibidem*, p. 240.
16. *Ibidem*, p. 437.
17. *Ibidem*, pp. 434, 436.
18. *Ibidem*, p. 432.
19. *Ibidem*, p. 368.
20. *Ibidem*, p. 255.
21. *Ibidem*, p. 278.
22. *Ibidem*, p. 600.
23. *Ibidem*, p. 255.
24. *Ibidem*, p. 600.
25. *Ibidem*, p. 256.
26. *The New Yorker*, July 10, 1971.
27. *The Pentagon Papers*, p. 436.
28. In the words of Leslie H. Gelb: "The foreign-policy community had become a 'house without windows,'" *Life*, *op. cit.*
29. *The Pentagon Papers*, p. 438.
30. In Stavins, Barnet, Raskin, *op. cit.*, p. 209.
31. *The Pentagon Papers*, p. 438.
32. In Stavins, Barnet, Raskin, *op. cit.*, p. 24.
33. *The Pentagon Papers*, pp. 5 and 11.
34. *Ibidem*, p. 268.
35. *Ibidem*, pp. 334–335.
36. *Ibidem*, p. 16.
37. *Ibidem*, p. 15 ff.
38. *Ibidem*, p. 166.
39. *Ibidem*, p. 25.
40. Gelb, in *Foreign Policy*, *op. cit.*; Ellsberg, *op. cit.*
41. *The Pentagon Papers*, p. 313.
42. Maurice Laporte, *L'histoire de l'Okhrana*, Paris, 1935, p. 25.
43. *The Pentagon Papers*, p. 6.
44. *Ibidem*, pp. 253–254.
45. The Chicago *Sun-Times*, quoted by the New York *Times*, "The Week in Review," June 27, 1971.
46. *The Pentagon Papers*, p. 254.
47. *Ibidem*, p. 98.
48. *Ibidem*, p. 242.
49. Ellsberg, *op. cit.*, p. 247.
50. *The Pentagon Papers*, p. 433.
51. *Ibidem*, p. 240.

52. *Ibidem*, p. 407.
53. *Ibidem*, p. 583.
54. *Ibidem*, p. 342.
55. *Ibidem*, p. 414.
56. *Ibidem*, p. 584.
57. *Ibidem*, pp. 534–535.
58. *Ibidem*, p. 153.
59. *Ibidem*, p. 278.
60. *Ibidem*, pp. 4, 26.
61. The New York *Times*, June 29, 1971. Mr. Smith cites Professor Whiting's testimony before the Senate Foreign Relations Committee on the document, which appears in *Foreign Relations of the United States: Diplomatic Papers 1945*, Vol. VII: *The Far East, China*, Washington, D.C., 1969, p. 209.
62. Tom Wicker in The New York *Times*, July 8, 1971.
63. Barnet in Stavins, Barnet, Raskin, *op. cit.*, p. 246.
64. *The Pentagon Papers*, p. 2.
65. Ellsberg, *op. cit.*, p. 219.
66. *Ibidem*, p. 235.
67. Barnet in Stavins, Barnet, Raskin, *op. cit.*, p. 248.
68. *Op. cit.*, p. 263.
69. Barnet in Stavins, Barnet, Raskin, *op. cit.*, p. 209.
70. *The Pentagon Papers*, p. 576.
71. *Ibidem*, p. 575.
72. *Ibidem*, p. 98.
73. Leslie H. Gelb suggests in all earnestness that the mentality of "our leaders" was formed by "their own careers having been a series of successful gambles, they hoped they somehow could do it again in Vietnam." *Life, op. cit.*
74. Barnet in Stavins, Barnet, Raskin, *op. cit.*, p. 209.
75. *The Pentagon Papers*, pp. 5, 13.
76. *Ibidem*, p. xx.
77. *Ibidem*, p. xviii.
78. Barnet in Stavins, Barnet, Raskin, *op. cit.*, p. 212.
79. *The Pentagon Papers*, p. 241.
80. *Ibidem*, p. 469.
81. *Ibidem*, p. 312.
82. *Ibidem*, p. xviii.
83. *Ibidem*, p. ix.

84. *Der Spiegel*, Number 35, 1971.

85. Eugene Kinkead, "Reporter at Large," *The New Yorker*, October 26, 1957.

86. *The New Yorker*, September 4, 1971.

87. *Ibidem.*

ABOUT THE AUTHOR

HANNAH ARENDT was born on October 14, 1906, in a borough of Hanover, Germany, the only child of politically progressive and secular Jewish parents. At the University of Marburg, she studied philosophy under Martin Heidegger, whose thinking would exert a notable influence on her later work. Following her year at Marburg, she spent a semester at the University of Freiburg, before moving on to the University of Heidelberg, where in 1928 she earned a doctorate in philosophy at age twenty-two. Her dissertation on Augustine's concept of *caritas* (neighborly love) was written under the direction of Karl Jaspers. After Adolf Hitler came to power in 1933, Arendt, having been arrested briefly for illegal research into antisemitism, fled Nazi Germany and emigrated to Paris. In 1940, once again in flight from the Nazis, she left France and made her way to the United States by way of Portugal. In 1941, Arendt settled in New York, her primary residence for the remainder of her life, where she became part of an intellectual circle that included Mary McCarthy, Dwight Macdonald, Alfred Kazin, Lionel Trilling, and Delmore Schwartz. Arendt taught at various American universities, including Princeton, the University of Chicago, and

The New School for Social Research. Her major works of political thought were written after she became a naturalized U.S. citizen in 1950. In 1951, she published *The Origins of Totalitarianism*, a study of Nazi Germany and Stalinist Russia, followed in 1958 by *The Human Condition*, which offered a narrative of the modern age told through the human activities of labor, work, and action. Arendt also published a steady stream of literary and biographical essays and political journalism. Her best-known book, *Eichmann in Jerusalem* (1963, rev. 1964)—a portrait of Adolf Eichmann, a leading administrator of the Holocaust—came out of a series of articles written for *The New Yorker*. Her influential historical study *On Revolution* (1963) offered a comparative estimate of the American and French Revolutions. At the time of her death on December 4, 1975, of a heart attack, she was at work on a three-volume study, *The Life of the Mind*, on the faculties of thinking, willing, and judging.

Notes

Arendt's own notes for "Truth and Politics" and "Lying in Politics" appear immediately after the respective essays. The notes below are intended to provide readers with additional guidance. Reference numbers denote page and line of this volume (the line count includes headings).

TRUTH AND POLITICS

3.1   TRUTH AND POLITICS] First published in a slightly different form in *The New Yorker*, February 17, 1967; reprinted in *Between Past and Future: Eight Exercises in Political Thought* (New York: Viking, 1968).

5.9   "*Fiat veritas, et pereat mundus*"] Latin: Let truth be done, though the world may perish. Arendt twists the maxim "Fiat justitia, et pereat mundus," substituting "truth" for "justice."

5.10   even more implausible] Prior to the appearance of the 2006 Penguin Classics edition of *Between Past and Future*, all printings read "even more plausible." This corrected reading, courtesy of Jerome Kohn, is based on Arendt's drafts of *Between Past and Future* in the Hannah Arendt Papers at the Library of Congress.

6.17–18   "If they could . . . kill him,"] See Plato's *Republic*, book 7.

8.27–9.1   the role . . . history books—] Though he played an instrumental part in the 1917 overthrow of the Russian Provisional Government and the establishment of Vladimir Lenin's Communist regime, Leon Trotsky (1879–1940) found himself increasingly at odds with Joseph Stalin after Lenin's death and was forced into exile. Later, a systematic campaign to discredit Trotsky was undertaken in the Soviet Union, and Trotsky's achievements were expunged in a rewriting of Russian history. Trotsky was assassinated in 1940 in Mexico City by a Soviet agent.

11.19–20   "All governments . . . Madison said] See *The Federalist Papers*, No. 49: "If it be true that all governments rest on opinion, it is no less true that the strength of opinion in each individual, and its practical influence on his conduct, depend much on the number which he supposes to have entertained the same opinion."

12.16–18   "*Sage jeder . . . Gott empfohlen*"] From a letter by the German Enlightenment author Gotthold Ephraim Lessing (1729–1781) to J.A.H. Reimarus, April 6, 1778.

18.28–19.1   μετάβασις εἰς ἄλλο γένος] Greek: change into another genus.

22.13–15   "*Euclide est . . . véritablement despotiques.*"] French: Euclid is a true despot; and the geometric truths he passed on to us are truly despotic. Quoted from *L'Ordre naturel et essential des sociétés politiques* (1767) by Mercier de la Rivière.

22.15–18   Grotius, about . . . make four."] See Grotius's *On the Law of War and Peace* (1625), 1.1.10.5.

22.27   "*le pouvoir arrête le pouvoir*"] French: power stops power. See Montesquieu's *Spirit of the Laws* (1748), book 11, chapter 4.

28.2–3   Kant's categorical imperative] Fundamental principle of morality that the German philosopher Immanuel Kant (1724–1804), in one formulation, stated as: "Act only according to that maxim by which you can at the same time will that it should become a universal law."

30.5–8   Machiavelli recommended . . . they please"] See Machiavelli's *Discourses on Livy* (1531), book 3, chapter 1.

33.25   *imitatio Christi*] In Christian theology, the practice of following Christ's example.

46.19   Zinoviev, Kamenev, Rykov, Bukharin] Members of the Politburo and rivals of Joseph Stalin, all of whom were charged and executed on false evidence in the show trials of the 1930s.

48.17–21   "If falsehood . . . boundless field."] See "Of Liars" in Montaigne's *Essais* (1580).

54.8–9   "all sorrows . . . about them,"] Arendt also uses these words as an epigraph to the chapter on action in *The Human Condition* (1958). There, too, the quote is attributed to the Danish writer Isak Dinesen (1885–1962), but the source is unknown.

55.6–8   "at the end . . . of judgment."] See Isak Dinesen's "The Cardinal's First Tale" in *Last Tales* (New York: Random House, 1957).

LYING IN POLITICS

61.1   LYING IN POLITICS] First published in a slightly different form in *The New York Review of Books*, November 18, 1971, a little more than a year before all U.S. troops were withdrawn from Vietnam in January 1973 with the signing of the Paris Peace Accord; reprinted in *Crises of the Republic* (New York: Harcourt Brace Jovanovich, 1971).

61.3–8   "The Picture . . . ROBERT S. MCNAMARA] Quoted from a memo of May 19, 1967, by Secretary of Defense Robert S. McNamara to President Lyndon B. Johnson. Increasingly skeptical of U.S. involvement in the Vietnam War, for which he had been a chief architect, McNamara (1916–2009) resigned as secretary of defense in February 1968—a position held by him since his appointment by President John F. Kennedy in 1961.

61.10–17   THE PENTAGON PAPERS . . . May 1968] In 1971, the Pentagon Papers, officially the "Report of the Office of the Secretary of Defense Vietnam Task Force," were leaked to *The New York Times* and other newspapers by Daniel Ellsberg (b. 1931), a RAND Corporation employee who had worked on the study. On June 13, 1971, *The New York Times* ran the first of nine excerpts from the Pentagon Papers.

62.4   *The Pentagon Papers*] Neil Sheehan, et al. *The Pentagon Papers: As Published by The New York Times* (New York: Bantam, 1971).

68.9   Richard J. Barnet] Cofounder, with Marcus Raskin, of the progressive Washington, D.C. think tank the Institute for Policy Studies. His articles in opposition to the Vietnam War found outlets in *The New Yorker*, *Harper's*, *The Nation*, and elsewhere.

69.2   Neil Sheehan's] Cornelius Mahony Sheehan (1936–2001), *New York Times* reporter who first obtained the classified Pentagon papers.

73.17   The Tonkin incident] The U.S. destroyer *Maddox* was said to have been attacked by North Vietnamese torpedo boats in the Gulf of Tonkin on August 2, 1964, and a second attack on the *Maddox* and another destroyer, *Turner Joy*, was reported on August 4, on the doubtful evidence of "ghost" radar contacts. President Lyndon B. Johnson used the attacks to secure congressional approval of a resolution authorizing "all necessary measures" to "prevent further aggression" in Southeast Asia.

74.4   Dean Rusk] David Dean Rusk (1909–1994) served as secretary of state under Presidents John F. Kennedy and Lyndon B. Johnson, from 1961 to 1968.

75.13   John T. McNaughton's] Assistant secretary of defense from 1964 to 1967 and Robert McNamara's closest advisor and right-hand man. McNaughton died in a plane crash in 1967 shortly after being confirmed as secretary of the navy by the U.S. Senate.

76.15   Walt Rostow's] Walt Whitman Rostow (1916–2003), national security advisor to President Lyndon B. Johnson, from 1966 to 1969, and a leading strategist of the Vietnam War.

78.26–27   *Washington Plans an Aggressive War*] Ralph Stavins, Richard J. Barnet, and Marcus G. Raskin, *Washington Plans an Aggressive War: A Documented Account of the United States Adventure in Indochina* (New York: Random House, 1971).

81.2–3   Colonel Edward Lansdale] Edward Geary Lansdale (1908–1987), who had served with the Office of Strategic Services in World War II, was sent to Saigon in 1954 to head up the CIA's covert Saigon Military Mission.

81.14–15   the overthrow . . . Ngo Dinh Diem] In the late summer and fall of 1963 the Kennedy administration lost confidence in the ability of President Ngo Dinh Diem to prevent a Communist takeover in South Vietnam and to pacify Buddhist opposition to his rule. Through a CIA intermediary, the administration secretly informed generals plotting to overthrow Diem that the United States would not oppose a coup. On November 1, 1963, a group of military commanders ousted Diem, and on November 2 Diem and his brother Ngo Dinh Nhu were murdered by army officers acting on orders from one of the coup leaders.

82.26   agents of the Okhrana] Prerevolutionary tsarist secret police created to penetrate revolutionary organizations, including the Bolsheviks.

83.27   Rostow and . . . Taylor] Walt W. Rostow, see note 76.15. Maxwell Davenport Taylor (1901–1987) was chairman of the Joint Chiefs of Staff (1962–1964), ambassador to Vietnam (1964–1965), and special consultant to President Lyndon B. Johnson (1965–1969).

84.16–17   Senator Mike Mansfield] Michael Joseph Mansfield (1903–2001), American Democratic politician and Senate majority leader (1961–1977).

84.23   The bombing of North Vietnam] In 1965, President Lyndon B. Johnson authorized Operation Rolling Thunder, a heavy bombing campaign against North Vietnam, and the deployment of 175,000 troops to South Vietnam when it became clear Rolling Thunder had failed to deter the North Vietnamese.

86.14   George Ball . . . 1965] George Ball (1909–1994), undersecretary of state, warned President Lyndon B. Johnson in a memorandum of July 1, 1965: "The South Vietnamese are losing the war to the Viet Cong. No one can assure you that we can beat the Viet Cong or even force them to the conference table on our terms, no matter how many hundred thousand *white, foreign* (U.S.) troops we deploy." That memorandum made its way into the Pentagon papers.

88.2–8   Ho Chi Minh . . . Indochina"] In 1945, Japan overthrew Indochina's French colonial rulers and as a consequence Ho Chi Minh proclaimed Vietnamese independence; however, France refused to relinquish control of its former colony, thus initiating the First Indochina War (1946–1954).

90.13   *arcana imperii*] Latin: state secrets.

92.7–8   "Greek tragedy (proposed by Max Frankel and Leslie H. Gelb)] In a *New York Times* article of July 6, 1971, Max Frankel wrote: "So whatever its shortcomings, [the Pentagon papers] will stand as a vast trove of insights, hindsights and revelations about the plans and conceptions of small groups of men as they guided the nation into a distant but grievous venture, about how they talked and wrote to each other, to friend and foe, in public and in private. And the study is bound to stand as a new model for governmental analysis, raising questions normally reserved for literature. . . . As the coordinator of the Pentagon study, Leslie H. Gelb, recently said of this story, 'It was and is a Greek tragedy.'"

92.15–16 Mr. Nixon's metaphor . . . helpless giant"] Announcing a U.S. incursion into Cambodia on April 30, 1970, President Richard M. Nixon said: "If, when the chips are down, the world's most powerful nation, the United States of America, acts like a pitiful, helpless giant, the forces of totalitarianism and anarchy will threaten free nations and free institutions throughout the world."

100.11 Diem] See note 81.14–15.

101.15 Bernard Fall] Bernard B. Fall (1926–1967), war correspondent and political scientist whose academic analyses of Indochina were combined with a soldier's point of view and considerable experience on the ground. On February 21, 1967, he was killed by a land mine near Hue, in South Vietnam.

103.21–23 The Truman Doctrine . . . Gelb has pointed out.] Leslie H. Gelb, "Vietnam: The System Worked," *Foreign Policy*, no. 3 (1971): 140–67.

105.24–25 Pax Americana . . . Kennedy had denounced.] In a commencement address at American University, Washington, D.C., on June 10, 1963, President John F. Kennedy addressed the topic of "world peace": "What kind of peace do I mean? What kind of peace do we seek? Not a Pax Americana enforced on the world by American weapons of war. Not the peace of the grave or the security of the slave. I am talking about genuine peace, the kind of peace that makes life on earth worth living, the kind that enables men and nations to grow and to hope and to build a better life for their children—not merely peace for Americans but peace for all men and women—not merely peace in our time but peace for all time."

This book is set in 10½ point Minion Pro, a digital typeface designed by American typographer Robert Slimbach in 1990 for Adobe Systems and inspired by Renaissance-era fonts. The name comes from the traditional nomenclature for type sizes, the smallest of which was diamond, followed by pearl, agate, nonpareil, minion, brevier, bourgeois, long primer, small pica, pica, etc. The display type is a new sans serif font, Praktika, released in 2017 by Finnish designer and illustrator Emil Bertell and modeled after the early-twentieth-century grotesque typefaces used in European road signs.

The paper is acid-free and exceeds the requirements for permanence established by the American National Standards Institute.

Text design and composition by Gopa & Ted2, Inc., Albuquerque, NM.
Printing by Sheridan, Saline, MI.